Praise for *Break Loose and Fly*

"Kerstin Decook's book, *Break Loose and Fly,* will show you that you can overcome any obstacle and live the life of your dreams. Kerstin has learned a great deal from the trials and tribulations in her own life. If you want a book with a great story that is uplifting, inspiring, and filled with practical tools that you can use right away to improve your own life, this is the book for you."

— Neal Abramson, author of *You Can Choose Your Life: A Guide to Experiencing More Peace, Freedom, and Happiness Right Now*

"*Break Loose and Fly* provides a practical toolkit on how to change your thinking, and ultimately your life. Kerstin's personal journey offers inspiration and a promise that real and lasting change is possible."

— Daniel Macca MBA, PCC professional coach and consultant

BREAK
LOOSE
AND FLY

10 PRACTICAL TOOLS
FOR MASTERING
LIFE'S CHALLENGES
AND CREATING
A LIFE YOU'LL LOVE

KERSTIN DECOOK

Published by: Capucia, LLC
211 Pauline Drive #513
York, PA 17402

Paperback ISBN: 978-1-954920-09-5
eBook ISBN: 978-1-954920-10-1
Library of Congress Control Number: 2021911556

Cover Design: Ranilo Cabo
Layout: Ranilo Cabo
Illustrations Artist: Yvette Gilbert from the United Kingdom
Editor and Proofreader: Chrissy Das
Book Midwife: Carrie Jareed

Printed in the United States of America

DEDICATION

I am dedicating this book to you, my dear reader, because YOU MATTER!

I truly believe YOU CAN create and experience the life of your choosing and break through the barriers that hold you back from living an amazing life. I believe YOU CAN transform yourself into a confident, courageous, thriving, inspired, positive, adventurous, and successful individual.

I wrote this book to help you get unstuck and explore all the opportunities that lie ahead so **YOU CAN BREAK LOOSE**, become the person you are meant to be, **AND FLY** confidently in the direction of your dreams.

ACKNOWLEDGMENTS

Never in my wildest dreams did I ever think I would write a book one day, especially in a second language. But I did, and it's been an amazing and exciting journey full of adventure, insights, and aha moments.

I have so much gratitude for the people who've helped me behind-the-scenes and in one way or another touched, inspired, and enhanced this book.

First, I'd like to thank Jack, my ever-so-loving husband, for encouraging and endlessly supporting me in writing and birthing this book. He stood by my side from day one, lifted me up when I doubted myself, let me write when there was work to be done at home or in our business, suffered through countless hours of editing chapters that sometimes resembled a knock-down-drag-out fight over how to say things. I'll never forget when Jack read my first chapter and lovingly told me it was crap and that I needed to re-write it. What a start, huh? He also prepared dinner when I was too tired to cook. Thank you, Jack, for all your support and for always pushing me to be the best I can possibly be, whether as the author of this book or the first mate on our boat. I love you to the moon and back.

Next, I'd like to thank my dear friends and coaching colleagues, Wai Petersen, Dara Ayres, and Dick Cathell, for taking the time to read through each chapter and give me constructive feedback, ideas, and suggestions. I am so grateful for all the time you each devoted to my project knowing how busy your own worlds are. Thank you from the bottom of my heart!

A special thank you goes to the amazingly talented artist Yvette Gilbert from the United Kingdom, who made my illustration ideas for each chapter come to life. She worked collaboratively as a team to complete the work as I envisioned it and delivered beyond my greatest expectations. I had so much fun working with you, Yvette. I'm grateful for having found you on Fiverr.

I'd like to thank my daughter, Alicia Lycan, for doing a preliminary edit and polishing up my manuscript before I sent it to the publisher. I gave her short notice and a tight timeframe through which she pushed through like a pro! Thanks, honey for helping me with grammar and word choices. You are so talented in so many ways! I am proud to be your mom!

I'd also like to thank my mother for always supporting and believing in me. You've instilled in me a sense of worthiness and that I am stronger than I think and can do anything I put my mind to. Thanks, mom, for being my backbone and for letting me live my dreams for as long as I can remember.

Last, but not least, I'd like to thank the Capucia Publishing Team for guiding me through the publishing process one step at the time and supporting me along the way, no matter what roadblocks showed up. Carrie, Chrissy, Christine, Karen, Jean, Penny, Corinne, Lauren and the rest of your amazing team, you've all been so wonderful to work with.

CONTENTS

Introduction   1

Chapter 1
Dream up your amazing life so you can have one   5

Chapter 2
Wake up the lion in you   21

Chapter 3
Harness the power of your mind   37

Chapter 4
Focus on the target no matter what gets in your way   55

Chapter 5
Align yourself with your values   79

Chapter 6
Conquer anxiety and experience inner peace   101

Chapter 7
Free yourself from emotional baggage   121

Chapter 8
Discover the transformative power of "Energy Leadership"   145

Chapter 9
Set yourself up for success   163

Chapter 10
Never Stop Listening, Learning, and Growing   185

Appendix   207

Resources   209

About the Author   211

Break Loose and Fly Coaching   213

INTRODUCTION

I lived the first 16 years of my life behind the "Iron Curtain" in Russian-occupied Eastern Germany where we could not say or do anything that wasn't approved by the government and life was marked by scarcity of even the simplest things. I was stuck in what seemed to be a depressing and hopeless situation, but when I began to dream of possibilities instead of dwelling on the tyrannical and oppressive life I led, my life changed.

While most of us would like to break loose and fly in the direction of our dreams, many of us think it's not possible. We have different reasons for thinking this way—whether it's our upbringing, past experiences, or current circumstances. It's understandable we think and feel the way we do. However, I truly believe it is possible for each and every one of us to break loose and fly. If you think you can't, look at the gravity-defying flight of the bumblebee. It teaches us every day that the seemingly impossible is possible. Based on the laws of aerodynamics, the bumblebee should not be able to fly as its body is too heavy for its wings. The bumblebee, being unaware of these scientific facts, flies anyway.

The lesson of the bumblebee captures the story of my life. I have learned to fly against all odds. I still crash once in a while, but the sheer joy of being able to spread my wings and fly every so often inspires me to get up in the morning and look forward to what the day holds in store for me. My wish and hope for you is to think and feel the same way. That is why I wrote this book for you.

About two years ago, an email popped up in my inbox from a friend I hadn't heard from for nearly twenty years. He wrote:

"Hi Kerstin, it seems you have figured things out, how to deal with and overcome challenges, failures, pitfalls and defeat, and turn those into something positive making you look so happy and content. I wish I had the courage, confidence, and adventurousness to do the same…"

Wow, what a statement. His words stuck with me. As I was sitting there staring at my computer and the email, my mind flashed back to all of the challenges I had encountered thus far and the many mistakes I had made. So many, in fact, I can't even count them. Let me rephrase that—rather than calling those "mistakes," let's call them "choices." I made some choices that turned out to be great and others that tested me to my limits. I managed to navigate through them, but it was neither easy nor painless.

The accumulated choices in my life brought me to where I am today, and the lessons I've learned from them have made me the strong person I am. Now, I'm able to navigate through challenges quicker and with less pain, but it's an ongoing effort requiring my full commitment and willingness to push through the challenges and look for solutions. Challenges aren't problems that will solve themselves somehow. I've learned to leap into the unknown to figure things out and not let fear hold me back. Fear is one of the greatest battles we all fight and desire to overcome. I am not exempt from it. We need to understand fear separates us from success, prosperity and abundance. It also prevents us from achieving our full potential and living the life we are meant to live. The life we desire is on the other side of fear, and greatness awaits over there.

The question is: how do we get to the other side and overcome the fears that are holding us hostage? This book is designed to help you answer that question so you can not only push past fear, but conquer it, too!

How about you, my dear reader? What does your life look like right now? How do you feel about the decisions and choices you've made so far?

Chances are, if you are reading this book, you want to live your life differently. You may be looking back at the choices and decisions you've made in the past thinking, *I am always making the wrong choice and life sucks, because there is one challenge after another.* Maybe you feel a choice you made long ago is still haunting you and continuing to cause grief and pain that just won't subside. You can't really move on, because that issue is bogging you down and weighing heavily on your shoulders.

Perhaps you feel like it's difficult for you to even make a choice. You like to hold onto what's familiar, because you feel comfortable there, even though it sucks because life is happening all around you. By staying in your comfort zone, it becomes more and more difficult to step out into the unknown.

Maybe you'd much rather have more courage to take more chances, but you don't because you could fail. Why would you subject yourself to failure, anyways? You might be dealing with fear of success and the changes that may result. You might wonder if you are up to the task or fear how others may react to your success. Will there be jealousy or resentment?

I get it, these are all valid thoughts and feelings. It's understandable to feel disappointed, frustrated, hurt, or bummed when life seems unfair or difficult and you feel you can't overcome the fear, grief, pain, or anxiety facing you.

Does any of this ring true for you? If so, keep reading. And know you are not alone—many people think and feel the same. If you want

3

more from your life or feel your life is just not hitting the mark, I invite you to read on and discover ten tools that will help you make a meaningful change so you can live life to the fullest, enjoy the journey, and thrive. If you don't know yet what the life you love even looks like, let's see if together we can shed some light onto this vision for you. Let's see and explore some of the opportunities that are available to you so YOU CAN break loose, become the person you are meant to be, and fly confidently in the direction of your dreams. To get the most out of this book, I encourage you to follow the action steps and actively participate. After all, you bought this book to explore how you can master life's challenges and create an amazing life, wouldn't you agree? I applaud you for having great intentions…now we just need to get you moving and turn your intentions into actions, so you actually get the results you desire. Working through the action steps will enhance the journey for you and ultimately get you closer to the amazing life you wish to live. With every tool you implement, you can take your life from the ordinary to extraordinary. The more you choose to adapt, the greater the extraordinary can be. It's your choice!

Let's go. Life is precious. You only get to live once! Just because it has not been as great as you wish doesn't mean the future has to be the same. Every new day is a chance to change your life! I am not saying it's easy, but YOU CAN DO IT if you really want to. I would love to help you find a way to live a life that you truly love!

To your amazing life!
Kerstin

4

CHAPTER 1

Dream up your amazing life so you can have one

Imagine the melodic song of a beautiful little canary bird. How beautiful, how precious. That's the reason why many people desire and purchase canaries—for their attractive, sweet-sounding song. Did you know the canary is a domesticated form of a wild songbird in the finch family that originated in the Macaronesian Islands? The Macaronesian Islands are entirely volcanic and located in the North Atlantic Ocean off the coast of Europe and Africa. The islands share a gentle climate and offer a wide variety of landscapes, beautiful mountains, cliffs, valleys, and sheltered bays. If I could live there, I'd probably sing all day long, too. Life in a cage is quite different, yet canaries continue to sing; this is why we love them so much.

Growing up in Russian-occupied Eastern Germany, I felt very much like a canary bird stuck in a cage. Depending on your age, you may or may not know anything about the GDR (German Democratic Republic), also known as East Germany, which was formed in 1949. After World War II, Russia gained control of the eastern half of Germany. A communist system was established, which was led by Commanders who were trained in the Soviet Union under Joseph Stalin's principles. Those Commanders ran the country following Russia's Communist guidelines to the highest degree! The commanding officers dictated our lives. They told everyone what to do. Freedom of speech or the freedom to do what you wanted did not exist. Your friends and neighbors were ordered to spy on you and everyone else as part of being a good citizen.

Besides that, the general living conditions were extremely poor. Buying basic food, clothing, or anything else was nearly impossible unless you had connections. The conditions were so bad that thousands of East Germans escaped to West Germany, because life was much better there and not under socialist rule. In response to those escapes, the Communist East German authorities fixed this problem in 1961 by building a wall—literally thrown up overnight. The wall effectively caged everyone who lived in the eastern part of Germany. Those who tried to escape were brutally shot. There was no more traveling "outside" allowed.

This is where my story begins. I was born on the wrong side of the wall, in captivity. My parents owned a bakery, which closed when I was just a year old because my father decided to leave with the assistant who was hired to support my mom while she took care of my sister and me and managed the bakery at the same time. While my father created a new family, mom went back to her old job as an x-ray technician and tried her best to give my sister and me a good life. Even though I was a creative, audacious kid and enjoyed playing with my friends, I felt stuck and life was depressing for the most part.

There was nothing I could do about the fields of gray we lived in. Gray streets, gray houses, gray air, gray everything! There was no color anywhere because our leaders thought we didn't need or deserve paint, or anything else for that matter. As time passed, the paint on all of the stone buildings peeled away and all that was left was gray concrete. If things weren't gray, they were pale at best—like pale green bananas that tasted like glue, or unripened oranges that tasted like straw, or the greenish and partially rotten potatoes that dripped through the bag while you carried them home from the grocery store. Yuck!

And then there were lines for anything you needed to survive or desired to enjoy life. Long lines of people waited in rain, frost, and snow for whatever was left to be sold at the end. If you saw a line, you lined up. That was the drill, whether you knew what was being sold or not. If you could not use it, perhaps a friend could. When the lines would disband as the product sold out, the rest would all go home empty-handed.

I resented the lines as much as the three-story shithole we lived in. Our flat was on the first floor. It had an unheated outside toilet and community bath with no hot running water. Mom had to heat up the water with a coal-fired stove before she could give us a bath. Thinking that our neighbors bathed in there before us was a revolting thought, but we all shared the one and only tub in the house. Other than on "bath days," we would wash ourselves in the kitchen sink.

The flat had no electric heat, thus we needed to bring coals up from the cellar to heat the stoves. Coals up and ashes down the frigid concrete steps, day-in and day-out, throughout the coldest months of the year. Since I was stronger than my sister, it was my job for the most part.

I resented that life was so challenging. Mother struggled to dress us and put food on the table. My father paid very little alimony. Not only was it difficult financially, but things were rare, and, without connections, you could not get much of anything. One shirt for all, in all sizes, yoo-hoo.

Imagine this.

People who wanted and could afford a car had to put their names on the waiting list for over 10 years. Yes, *years,* not months, just to get one of the junkiest cars ever made in history, a "Trabant" (which we called "Trabi"). That thing was made of duroplast, a recycled cotton waste from the Soviet Union and phenol resins from the East German dye industry. Yabba dabba doo, as Fred Flintstone would say. The Trabi was as loud as a tractor, smoked like a chimney, and cost more than an entire year's wages for a typical worker. For those who could afford one, all that mattered was they could drive instead of walk.

You simply could not go to the store to buy what you needed, whether it was a washing machine, television, coffee maker, shoes in your size, whipping cream for birthday cakes, or the meat of your choice when you wanted to cook something special for visitors. Meal planning in general was not an option, because you'd never know what you could get your hands on. We always joked when going to the butcher shop, as it appeared they sold tile rather than meat. Most of the time, all you could see were floor-to-ceiling tiled walls with empty meat hangers and a few shriveled-up sausages on the shelves. The butcher shops were open anyway. How ironic.

Having to live like that sucked, but what was even more depressing was the fact that we were told what to do and how to think. Let me rephrase that. Thinking for ourselves was not an option at all. We had to recite what we were told, children and adults alike. While children recited the hymns that were drilled into us to brainwash our little minds, the doctors at my mom's hospital were ordered to tell patients that Cadmium is not dangerous to the human body. Seriously? We were told the Soviet Union was our best friend. What a joke!

Would a best friend let us live like that? Would a best friend make school-aged children work in factories one day a week? Kids had to wear work suits with hairnets while working on machines or making parts for whatever…we did not know. It was all about creating brainless worker bees that would do as they were told and produce for the "fatherland." While "In God We Trust" is the official motto of the United States of America, we were told: "We don't need sunshine nor the Lord."

Sadly, most people accepted the way things were in order to survive. They learned to cheer for our leaders who made everyone march in parades past their podium while singing and waving. Not so for my mom, nor me and my sister. Mother did not share the same principles and would not allow us to curse the god we prayed to. She would not compromise her faith just because life would have been easier to do so. Those who followed our leaders would be rewarded; those who opposed would feel the consequences.

And so it was. My sister and I were outsiders in school.

We were not able to participate in any school activities because we did not belong to the Pioneers or the FDJ (Free German Youth). These organizations would drill the socialist ideology into children and youth, turning them into little robots early on in life. We were not able to go to music school because we did not swing our hat to "the king."

Even though our flat had no electric heat or a bathroom or hot running water, we did not have the privilege of moving to a newer apartment like others because my mother didn't adhere to the rules of attendance and participation set by our leaders. When mom applied for new housing—just imagine, you had to "apply"—two men came to inspect our flat, stomped on the floor, approved the condition, and that was it. They left saying there was no reason for us "needing" to move. We "wanted" to move, but "wanting" anything was not an option for us.

We were victims to a huge extent, yet mother kept fighting to provide us a better future with God in our lives. This was dangerous. It could have gotten her thrown in jail. My sister and I could have been put in an orphanage or given to the father who did not want us. While my sister and I didn't like being outsiders, mom explained why it's important in life to never compromise your values for anybody or anything or you just turn into a puppet, worse it can have a detrimental effect on your well-being. She kept a positive attitude through all the challenges we experienced and tried wholeheartedly to bring joy to our lives as much as she could. Mom organized fun birthday parties and the best vacation time we could have under the circumstances. She let us have sleepovers, paid for private music lessons, and signed us up for church events whenever possible.

Mother gave her all to provide us the most wonderful childhood, but there was nothing she could do about the external circumstances. We were stuck in this life. It felt like we were living in prison and nothing would ever change. We were held hostage and told what to do. Having little control over how we lived our lives was the biggest challenge for most of us. Some could not handle it and gave up. One of our neighbors and my sister's best girlfriend both committed suicide by jumping out of a three-story building. Sadly, one of my girlfriends jumped, too. It did not kill her, but left her crippled for the rest of her life. It was as painful to witness as it was to live this life in captivity.

Since there was nothing I could do about the depressing external world I was living in, I decided to change my internal world and turn the gray days into colorful, vibrant stories. As often as I could, I escaped to fantasy land and dreamed that one day things would be different, and I would be free to fly high in the sky long before I was too old to do so. Dreamland was a place to retreat to when I felt bummed, sad, angry, and frustrated. Every time I went to Dreamland, I felt free from the constraints I experienced in my everyday life. I can't say in particular why, but I had big and audacious dreams.

We were not allowed to travel outside of Germany, so I dreamed about New Zealand and Canada, just because those countries sounded intriguing and far, far away. I dreamed about living there one day, free to do what I wanted to do. I listened to the adventures of "Alfons Wobblecheek" and other fantasy stories on old records and imagined someday I too would have an adventure in one of those places. When I shared my dreams with some of my friends, they would laugh because there was "no way" this would ever happen. "Don't you know that we live behind walls?" they would ask. "We can't go anywhere, just accept it and let it be."

Well, I was not going to do that. It sounded hopeless. Without hope, what's the point of getting out of bed every day?

It was the dreaming, my flights to fantasy land, that kept me in a happy place when skies were gray and life seemed unfair, when the days were dull and the bread was stale, when mom could not find me shoes that I desperately needed, when I could not participate in my classmates' activity because I was not a Pioneer, or when my classmates called me names because I was indeed an outsider. When life was out of my control, I went to my happy place and started singing and dreaming, just like the canary bird who sings even when held in a cage. It sings and sings and sings until it's last breath. I wasn't going to stop singing either. I love being alive no matter how hard things seem to be. *Someday, somewhere out there are possibilities for me. I just need to hold on to this dream and believe in it.* And so, I was dreaming that one day the door of the cage would open, and I could spread my wings and fly.

This "visioning" enabled me to overcome the feelings of being a victim. You may not recognize it, but there is immense freedom in dreaming up and imagining a better future for yourself. When you embark on flights to fantasy land, you are breaking through the barriers that hold you hostage. These barriers can be the circumstance itself, like living behind the wall or self-limiting beliefs, like thinking "nothing will ever change for me." We will discuss these limiting concepts and how to harness the power of your mind in the next two chapters.

11

I did not realize, when I escaped to Dreamland, that I had created a vision board in my mind. This is one of the most powerful tools we can use to attract the things we desire in our life. A vision board is a canvas or posterboard or piece of paper where you place your dreams, goals, and all the things you want and yearn for in your life. It represents your ideal life through images, pictures, words, inspirational quotes, and the like...whatever it is that you dream of or would like to achieve.

I didn't know about vision boards as a child, yet I had a very specific dream I continuously visualized. By doing so, I subconsciously began to create my future. By dreaming of and seeing a better tomorrow, not just once in a while, but all through my difficult childhood, I gave life to my current reality. As you will come to know later in this book, I immigrated to Canada and continue to live an adventurous life. The impossible became possible! It's amazing. My dreams have come true!

People in all walks of life use vision boards to help them achieve their goals. Olympic athletes use them to train and condition their minds to improve and maximize performance. They use visualization to condition their brain for a successful outcome. Books have been written about the power of visualization and "The Law of Attraction"—what you focus on expands! Visualization activates the creative powers of your subconscious mind and programs your brain to notice resources and opportunities that are available to you to help you achieve your goals.

Jack Canfield, co-author of the *Chicken Soup for the Soul* series, describes it this way: "Your brain will work tirelessly to achieve the statements you give your subconscious mind. And when those statements are the affirmations and images of your goals, you are destined to achieve them!" This has been true for me. I find this amazing and extremely powerful. Studies show that when athletes visualize a successful competition, they activate the same area of their brain that is stimulated as if they were physically performing that same action. And the more they mentally rehearsed their performance, the more it became habituated in their mind. Thus, guided imagery and visualization has become a part of elite sports training. If you like to learn more about these studies visit the Peak Performance Sports website at https://www.peaksports. com/sports-psychology-blog/. You and I may not be athletes, but that does not mean we can't tap into the same "source" and utilize the power of visualization to condition our brain for success.

Often in life, we can feel like victims to either our circumstances (like I did) or our thoughts, beliefs, emotions, and perceptions that hold us hostage and work against us. When we feel hopeless, worry, doubt, or our low self-esteem prevents us from doing something we know we want to do, life feels like a relentless struggle, with no way of escaping. It can be depressing.

But I'm thinking you bought this book because you don't want to be a victim anymore. Perhaps you want to find out how to create a life you will love and be happy with.

The life I'm living now started with a dream behind the walls of East Germany. Wherever you are right now, it can start for you, too.! To create and live an amazing life, you first have to clarify what you want your life to look like. A vision board is a great way to explore what you want, create the visual images for it, and look at it every day. It should represent all that you want in your life to feel happy and fulfilled. On that note, let me share with you tool #1...you may have guessed it already.

TOOL #1: Create A Vision Board

Clarifying your vision of your ideal life and business will help you to set goals that will get you from where you are now to where you want to be. With this clarity you can create an action plan and move in that direction. I will talk more about written goals and action plans in Chapter 9.

A vision board is different from written goals because it provides instant visual recognition of all that you desire and want to achieve—all in one place. Written goals need to be read word for word, which takes much more time than looking at the collection of images on your vision board and "visualizing" your future each day. There is an old saying, "A picture is worth a thousand words," which is true when using a vision board to lay out your goals and dreams. A vision board is that picture.

Your first thought might be: "Oh no, I have no idea what to put on there." One of my coaching clients, who is a man in his 50s, said the same thing. He thought his canvas would stay blank, but once he started, he was amazed and pleasantly surprised that in only one day his board had turned into a colorful collage of the things he wished for.

Perhaps you think this exercise is only for younger people who are still in the process of figuring out what they want to do with their lives and what it would take for them to be happy and fulfilled. Nope, not true! It does not matter how old you are, it's never too late to dream up how your amazing life would look like and then set goals and think of actions steps that will get you there. Just think of Colonel Harland David Sanders who did not believe that the future belongs to the young, as he started the Kentucky Fried Chicken franchise at the age of 65!

Maybe you're one of those people who thinks, "Oh no, I am not going to start dreaming about what I really want, because I can't have it anyway." I hear you, my friend. It's hard to believe anything when you feel stuck or "imprisoned" by whatever it may be. Many of us battle with self-limiting beliefs. The good news is that we can overcome those as you'll see in the next two chapters.

If the "oh no" thought is one that resides in your mind, I encourage you to give yourself a push and, as we would say in German, "jump over your own shadow." Give creating a vision board a try. What do you have to lose? Nobody is watching! Have some fun with this exercise, perhaps put music on or if you like to sing, keep chirping away as you start dreaming up a life that you would truly love and be happy with. What if you end up with a colorful collage, just like my client? Even if there is just one thing that comes to mind, whether a vacation or a job or house or a relationship, glue it on your board. It's a first step toward the amazing life that's waiting for you.

You can always add on. There are no rules as to how many dreams your vision board can hold. And for now, it does not matter whether you believe in the fact that what you wish for can happen for you. As I said, I'll get to the limiting beliefs that hold us hostage in the next chapters. For now, "No stinking thinking," my friend. This is Dreamland, not limitation land.

It doesn't take any more energy to create a big dream than it does to create a little one. Dream big, soar high, go far! The sky is not your limit. The limit is in your mind when you think it's impossible. Don't go there anymore. What if there is the slightest possibility for your dream to come true? That is what keeps me dreaming and what brings excitement to my life—the slightest possibility for my dreams to turn into reality one day. What would you think if your dreams came to life for you? Just imagine!

PUTTING THIS TOOL INTO ACTION

Here are some ideas that might help you create your vision board.

You've likely heard about the genie in the bottle from Disney's *Aladdin*. Well, pretend for a moment that you rubbed the magical oil lamp and the genie appeared to grant you not just three, but as many wishes as you'd like. Ask yourself, if you could do anything you wanted and had all the time, resources, talent, and self-confidence in the world, then:

- What would you do in your career?
- What would do for fun and enjoyment?
- Who would you become as a person?
- What would you have?
- Where would you live?
- What would your intimate relationships look like?
- What would your family/parenting life look like?
- What would your social life look like?
- What would your health/weight look like?

Whatever it is that you wish for, put it on your vision board. Have fun with it! Imagine...

When done, place your vision board somewhere you can see it daily, and take a few minutes each day to visualize your ideal life. This is important! Remember what elite athletes do! Daily visualization programs your brain to perceive and recognize available resources and opportunities that will help you to get closer to your dreams and goals. It also builds up your internal motivation to take the necessary actions to achieve your goals.

I like to think of our subconscious mind as a "radar antenna" that, when turned on, lets us see more of our surroundings that we can't see with the human eye. Activating the radar of your subconscious mind will enable you to see obstacles and opportunities just as a ship in the sea can find rocky shores and defined channels to enable it to get where it wants to go, even at zero visibility. Creating a higher level of awareness is the primary function of a vision board. Looking at your vision board and reviewing your goals and desires daily helps you to work through whatever hardships you are facing. It serves as a beacon to help you find your way, just as the mariners use lighthouses to find their way through difficult waters.

I created my first vision board about twelve years ago. I had just gone through my second divorce and struggled with all the emotional and financial drama that comes with it. It's simply amazing how many things came alive for me after using the vision board tool. One of the things that I had not achieved, but always wanted in my life, was a partner I could share "meaningful moments" with—not just temporarily, but for as long as we both lived. I know, it sounds like a big stretch after two divorces. But just because it was not in my past did not mean that I could not have it in my future. I found a silhouette picture of a couple embracing each other with a beautiful sunset background, cut it out, glued it on my vision board and wrote "meaningful moments" beside it. This was a big dream and I am so thrilled that it came true for me (remember I mentioned Jack, my husband, who helped me with this book?). I want to add even more, dream bigger, and fly higher. It's simply magical what can happen when you start creating your dream life!

The vision board may seem frivolous, but it acts as an anchor for all the upcoming work. For that reason, I encourage you to start your vision board before moving on to the next chapter. Yes, it's tempting to skip this action step and keep on reading, but trust me, it's a powerful tool that will help you set a direction in which you would like to see your life move. So, no skipping. Stop reading (after the Action Step) and start dreaming!

Here is your ACTION STEP for this tool.
Use it now!

Put your imaginative hat on and create a Vision Board to clarify what you want your life to look like. Remember the genie that grants you all the wishes you make? Picture this happening to you...you rubbed the lamp and the genie appeared. Now you have the career of your dreams, do the activities you love and enjoy, have what you want, live where you want to live, enjoy the relationships you yearn for, feel great about your health and well-being, and have whatever else it is you wish to possess, achieve, and/or become. Let yourself have what you want, breathe into the possibilities, dream big, soar higher, and imagine the feeling of having what your heart desires.

You can use magazine or online images, cuttings, pictures, phrases, or words that represent how you want to feel—like happy, powerful, fearless, courageous, healthy, confident, and so forth. You can create your own drawings that remind you of your desired future or glue on any material you feel represents your ideal life, like sand and a shell for living in a beach house one day. Use colored pencils or pens if you like or whatever else your creative side decides is right. One word of caution though: Don't clutter up your vision board. Remember, the Law of Attraction states: What you focus on expands. I doubt that you want to attract clutter into your life.

When done, remember to place your vision board somewhere where you can see it every day to remind yourself regularly of what you want your life to look like and to let your "radar antenna" (your subconscious mind) find available resources and opportunities to help you get what you desire.

If you can dream it, you can do it.
~Walt Disney

CHAPTER 2

Wake up the lion in you

Mother gave her best effort to provide us with a better life, and she never stopped trying. When several countries, including the GDR, signed the Helsinki Declaration in 1977 (that reflected human rights and the free movement of people across borders), mother applied to move and leave the country two years later when the opportunity became real for us in East Germany. It was a brave decision to hand in the application. Most people didn't for fear of being reprimanded or worse, thrown in jail. For mom this was an opportunity, whether it would ever happen or not was not one of her worries nor did she fear the consequences of her action. It was an opportunity, thus she seized it!

Her willpower and persistence paid off in the long run. In 1984, we were granted permission to leave East Germany. This only happened because the country was bankrupt and received money from West Germany. Under the agreement, they would release all who had applied to leave over the past several years. Under pressure, they were forced to let us go, which they did with the utmost contempt. We were given 24 hours' notice, they took our identity cards away, and accompanied us with machine guns and guard dogs to the border. I was sixteen years old at the time, and it was frightening.

My dream of "being free" one day had come true, but it was scary. We marched forward into an unknown future and had no idea what was waiting for us on the other side. The bright lights, vibrant colors, and all the delicious looking food, the hustle and bustle at the train station in Hamburg, West Germany, amazed me as much as it made me sick to my stomach. It had been so hard for me to imagine such a world where "everything" existed. I tried to be joyful, but failed because stress and anxiety took over. How was I going to handle this?

School in this new free world was hard and brought me to tears nearly every day. We were outsiders again. Our strong Saxonian accent repelled not only my classmates, but also my teachers who told me to either speak "proper German" or to not speak at all. Next was the foreign language issue that required my sister and me to switch schools. If we wanted to move on to higher education, we had to speak at least one foreign language fluently. We knew Russian, so we had to move to the only school that offered it, which unfortunately was the furthest away from home. The commute required us to take a half-hour train ride and then walk through the forest for another 15 minutes. Not exactly very convenient, but we toughed it out, rain, frost, or snow. It often reminded me of the lines in East Germany, when we just lined up no matter how shitty the weather was. Most kids lived closer to the school and had bikes, cars, or got rides from their parents. We did not. It was not the end of the world, but it did get me down every so often.

Next was the "thinking" issue, something that was not allowed in East German schools. I was good at memorizing and reciting whatever we were told, but free thinking was not something I was accustomed to. When asked to write a book report or interpret a story in school, I struggled tremendously. I had no opinion or understanding of how to have an opinion, because I was trained by the system to repeat, not to think. All I believed was that life was one challenge after another. My classmates laughed as they had never heard such a thing as "having no opinion." Their reaction often took the wind out of my sails. "Poor dumb little Russian girl, what a pity, we can't be friends with her."

This was not how I envisioned being free. The cage had opened, but I was not able to fly at all. It felt like a heavy weight had been tied to my wings. Being called names and belittled did not exactly help my self-esteem. I did not think I was a dumb girl, but other people's thoughts and beliefs about me made me wonder whether there was some truth to it. I started to doubt my capacity to navigate through this new world and all the challenges that came with it. There was this little voice that would come to visit me nearly daily whispering, "You are not good enough for this western world, you are an 'Ossy' and always will be." "Ossy" was the slang word used for people coming from Eastern Germany.

Disappointed, frustrated, and a bit angry, I looked in the mirror one day and thought, "What? Is this what freedom to do what you want to do looks like? It can't be like this." I chose to fight and not give up even though the days were hard, and others belittled me. Feeling sorry for myself was not an option. My dream to be free one day, free from control, and free to do whatever I wanted had come true. I felt *the world should be my oyster now, that's all that matters and that's what I needed to focus on.* So, I decided, "Screw you all. I can, and I will, fight for myself," just like my mother. I decided to focus on what was ahead of me, not on the difficult and frustrating environment I was currently living in. I was not successful every day, the tears would still roll off my cheeks once in a while. But overall, I kept my focus on the possibilities not the challenges.

After graduating from high school, I struggled through college working toward a degree to become a social educator with a focus on rehabilitation for those with physical or mental disabilities. While attending college, I worked at the Hamburger Alsterdorf Institution assisting people with disabilities to help pay for my education and to gain experience. There were times I felt like giving up because studying full time and working morning, evening, and weekend shifts was tiring.

I did not have a car and had to use public transportation to get to the college and to work. It was a one-hour train ride and an additional 20-minute walk to school, and a 25-minute subway ride followed by a 10-minute walk to work. I was still living with my mother because I could not afford to live on my own. One day, I came home and told her I was going to take some time off to find myself. It was "in" in the late 80's, a trend a lot of young adults were following. Mother was dumbfounded. "You want to do what? What does that even mean wanting to find yourself, huh? Have you lost your face or any other body part? To me, you look quite put together, there is nothing missing. I suggest you look in the mirror and find out for yourself." She added that if I insisted on doing what's "in" just because others were doing it, it would not happen under her roof. End of story.

I went to the bathroom and looked in the mirror because she had made a good point. What was I going to look for? Well, it was nothing other than a break that I wanted. College was difficult and having to work at the same time made studying even more challenging for me. I have a lot of strengths, but studying is not one of them. *You are simply not smart enough to study and finish college* was what the voice that spoke through the mirror would tell me. *You never were a good learner, why keep on trying when it's not in you?* That is a point I thought, maybe it's really not in me. But then I thought, that's just an excuse for not wanting to continue the hard work. I wanted to escape the everyday battle, that sounded easier than hanging in there and pushing through. Thinking

I can't do it was actually easier than thinking *I can*, because that would have allowed me to quit, so I thought.

So, when I looked in the mirror, I could not help but smile. All I discovered is that I was lazy, as simple as that. I had not "lost myself"—I just wanted the easy way out. It's okay to feel that way, I told myself, but you can't let those feelings affect your actions. You are stronger than that. I made an agreement with myself that day, from that moment on, I would do my best to focus on "I can" and not listen to the voice anymore that would tell me otherwise, especially in situations when the going got tough.

I countered that voice in my head with "I can, and I will." I told that voice, "I can, and I will do whatever it takes, no matter if you think I can't. Stop criticizing me and beating me down. I will find my way and that's it, whether you like it or not." Interestingly enough, this thought became my kick-ass power statement that accompanied me all my life to this day. It has empowered me when facing challenges. In those situations, I would say it over and over again, which made me not only stronger and inspired confidence, but I started to believe that I truly can.

After graduating from college, I landed my first job as a social educator and division manager by harnessing that power statement "I can, and I will." I was very nervous going into the interview, and it did not help that the voice tried to put me down again, reminding me I was not good enough, too young, too inexperienced (I literally had NO experience for that position), too this, too that. It certainly did not help either that my interview consisted of five middle-aged guys sitting around the conference table. I felt like I was being tossed into the lion's cage. These guys tore me to pieces with their intimidating questions and told me quite frankly I was not a good fit for the position. They did not think a young female fit in a school with adults of a similar age who had learning disabilities and were rough around the edges.

Of course, they did not say it this way as they had to be careful not to discriminate. "It takes a certain kind of person," they said. Their provoking statements made me angry. Why the heck did you invite me for the interview, if you already had your mind made up about me? I did not say that out loud, but these were my thoughts. Perhaps they had to, to give all qualified applicants a chance. While they did their best to convince me I was not a good fit, I kept on telling myself, "I can and I will show them I am the right fit, that I am that kind of person." It was my attitude that impressed the men in the end. They woke up the "sleeping lion" in me and helped me to carry myself through the interview in a way that convinced them I had what it took. Against all odds, I left the room with a job offer.

I came to learn later in life that many personal development programs use the image of a cat looking in the mirror, seeing a lion reflected back. The idea behind this is that what you think about, comes about. The way you see yourself directs your attitude, shapes your character, and influences your performance. It plays a major role in determining who you become. The message in the image is that you can change your life by changing your thoughts and the way you see yourself. What and how you define yourself becomes key to determining who you become. It's a self-fulfilling prophecy. You can actually *create* yourself! I wanted to *find* myself, which makes me laugh these days. I don't think one will ever find oneself, but I do believe you can mold yourself into the best version you can possibly be.

Here is the challenge though: When you look at yourself lowly, like a human being that has no self-esteem, no courage to do things, no power to make any changes, especially in times that are challenging, you are defining yourself as a failure and loser. At times, you may feel like an ant, which can easily be crushed under someone's feet. Sadly, if you see yourself that way, it's likely you will become that way, easily crushable. By believing you are a victim with little hope when it comes to conquering challenges, you are allowing your character, attitude, and even your spirit to be shaped by that limiting belief. The image of the lion in the mirror embodies strength, the ability to fight, and to be resilient.

If you see yourself as a strong person with confidence, courage, and boldness to change the things that you want to change, you feel empowered to conquer challenges with bravery and are able to fight when faced with adversity. It builds the character and attitude of the lion within you. It encourages you to seek greatness and stretches your capacity. You will begin to think and carry yourself as a winner, taking on challenges with courage, and you will not be easily swayed by adversity.

Let me ask you, how do you see yourself?

Perhaps you feel like a lion when things are great and seem in order. But as soon as that changes and things fall apart, when things don't go the way you wished and hoped for, you feel defeated again. You look in the mirror and there is no lion. You see a person who can't handle challenges, conquer them, and move forward quickly. Those situations throw you off balance and wear you down to a frazzle. You wish you knew what to do, how to get yourself up and going again, but you have no idea. It can be depressing, and it's understandable to feel that way.

So, how can we move out of these situations quickly? We need to wake up the lion within us and give him life, all the time. If he goes to sleep, we can easily fall into a trap, doubting we are capable of conquering anything with bravery, and we become vulnerable. How can we wake up the lion and keep him from falling asleep? Let's look at tool #2.

TOOL #2: Use Positive Self-Affirmations Daily

Self-affirmations are positive statements or phrases that define you as you would like to be in the present tense. They are used to challenge the negative and unhelpful thoughts that our self-critical inner voice is whispering in our ear daily. We all have an inner voice that likes to beat us down, that lets us believe we are less than who we really are and incapable of achieving anything. Have you heard that voice in your head that tells you not to try or not to take the risk because you might fail, or you won't be effective, or you might get hurt or embarrassed and the likes? Do you know the voice that simply states you are just not good enough? In his book, *The Untethered Soul*, Michael Singer (2007) calls the inner critic voice "the annoying roommate in your head that never shuts up." Great analogy in my opinion. If we listen to our inner critic voice, we most likely won't try or take the risk, because our "annoying roommate" already told us we will fail, get hurt, or feel awkward.

We have to learn to detach ourselves from the voice that makes us think negatively about ourselves. That voice has no business to tell us what to think or do and how to lead our life! We need to build skills so we don't believe what our "annoying roommate" is telling us. It seems like it becomes second nature eventually, and we have to learn how to believe we are actually amazing and reteach ourselves so that becomes our new second nature. How can we do it?

The first step is becoming aware of the voice. An easy way is to give the voice a name. You may think this is silly, but please hear me out. By giving your inner critic voice a name, you can call it out whenever it talks to you. I call mine "Grinch," because it literally steals my joy and focuses on the negative. The next step is not to engage with your inner critic voice if it calls you. So, if your "roommate" shows up, you could say, "Hi Grinch, I appreciate the advice, but I am going to do this my way, so why don't you take a hike?" To get him to leave you alone, show him the door with a positive affirmation. If the "Grinch" tells you "You are too weak"—reply "I am strong!" This lessens his power over you and increases yours!

Affirmations help us maintain a positive self-view and gain or restore self-confidence. They boost our self-esteem and ultimately enable us to combat negative patterns we fall back on when faced with adversity. Again, something I did not know back in my earlier days, yet I had made up my own affirmation. It worked for me all through my life and even today as I am writing this book.

If you are not used to using positive affirmations in your life and telling yourself how wonderful, powerful, and capable you are, it can seem a bit awkward at first. But bear with me. I can attest out of my own experience, they are powerful. People use them all over the world in all walks of life, just like vision boards. The concept of "what you focus on expands" applies to affirmations, too. We used them in our weekly real estate team meetings to kick-ass. It put a big smile on my face when, on the day I left my team to venture into a new business endeavor, they surprised me with a picture frame featuring my favorite kick-ass affirmation "I can, and I will," which presently hangs in my home office.

Now, that we've talked about affirmations in general, let's investigate how we can put them into practice.

PUTTING THIS TOOL INTO ACTION

Affirmations are a proven method of self-improvement and most powerful when practiced daily, especially when starting out as you prime your brain to the belief of your statements. Back in school, I repeated

"I can, and I will" more times a day than I can count. It turned into a habit that stayed with me all these years. It fuels me and empowers me to fight for myself, especially when facing adversity. It's a great habit to establish and to put in your toolbox for life.

Talking about habits, let me quickly touch on habits and habitual tendencies because they are so powerful. They shape our life more than we realize. We all have developed habits or tendencies over the course of our life, which means we've acquired routines or behaviors that have become nearly or completely involuntary and more automatic with each repetition. The question is whether those routines and behaviors work for us or against us. That's why we need to take control of our habits and tendencies and make sure we establish "the right ones" that will create a positive change for us and our life and let go of the "bad ones" that don't serve us well. The good news is that habits and habitual tendencies are not written in stone...they can be changed and replaced.

Positive affirmations fall into the "great habit to have" category as they work to our advantage and help us to create a positive change for our life. Dr. Carmen Harra, a renowned intuitive psychologist, best-selling author, radio show host, relationship expert, and TV personality states "When we verbally affirm our dreams and ambitions, we are instantly empowered with a deep sense of reassurance that our wishful words will become reality." I use positive affirmations all the time. When the going gets tough and I need to push through, I use my kick-ass power statement "I can, and I will". On a regular day-to-day basis, I use affirmations depending on the circumstances and goals that I am focusing on. Let me share some with you, so you get a better idea of their effectiveness.

Affirmations are stated in positive and present tense, in the here and now. They don't declare something you want; they state something you already believe you have. That's the way our subconscious mind works. When saying "I am…" you state it as if it's already true and your brain will work hard to make this a reality. Here are some of my positive affirmations:

- I am in control of my time and my habits.
- I am strong and in control of what I am feeding my body.
- I am able to conquer challenges with courage and confidence
- I am a powerhouse and can do anything I put my mind to.
- I am capable, talented, confident and possess the qualities needed to be successful.
- I am organized and strategic as to how I get things done.
- I can, and I will.

You can say your affirmations out loud every day, or you can write them down. I write mine down each morning in my five-minute journal book together with the goals I have for the day and three things I am grateful for. I will talk more about that later.

Affirmations help you gain confidence. When you convince yourself you are strong, you can do whatever it takes, you are talented, smart, creative, adventurous, and whatever else it is you want to be, your actions will follow from that belief. Confidence is a feeling of certainty. When you choose confident words, like "can, will, absolutely, certainly," and the like, you are literally talking yourself into a state of confidence. Sadly, it works the other way around, too.

If you doubt yourself and believe the inner critic voice that tells you "You can't" or you are too this or too that, you are talking yourself into a state of incompetence. Let's not go there. Claim confidence. You can do it! Affirmations will help you to "fake it until you make it" especially when you say them out loud. It's important to put your body in a state of confidence when saying your affirmations out loud. Yes, body language matters! So, use a confident stance: stand up tall, bring your shoulders back, take a deep breath, smile and say your affirmation with conviction! That's how you wake up that lion in you!

Which affirmation would work for you right now as you are reading this chapter? You can think of a specific goal you want to focus on like losing weight. Many of us deal with this challenge, I consistently do! For that challenge, you could use the statement "I am in control of my actions and capable of restricting my food intake," or something like that. Sometimes I repeat one affirmation for days to help myself concentrate on my goal and to focus on the fact I am truly capable of making a change.

Things will not change overnight, though. You can't become a high-performing athlete by practicing once a week. It takes time to build up muscles and get stronger. You have to put your best effort into it and practice daily, especially when just starting out. Waking the lion in you is the first step, keeping him alive and well cared for is an ongoing mission. By reading this book, the chances are you're interested in creating a life you feel good about and finding ways to conquer challenges with courage and confidence. Affirmations are one of the tools that can help you achieve where you want to be. I encourage you to practice affirmations daily, until they become a habit. This is one time when talking to yourself is acceptable. You might be amazed to see "the stronger version of yourself" more often reflected back in the mirror!

"Affirmations boost our self-esteem and ultimately enable us to combat negative patterns we fall back on when faced with adversity."

~Kerstin Decook

Here is your ACTION STEP for this tool.
Use it now!

Give your inner critic voice a name.
Write it down here: *Nancy*
_____

Think of a negative or unhelpful thought that it likes to whisper in your ear often. What is it that he/she likes to tell you? Write it down here: *You are not good enough.*

Now think what is the opposite of that negative whisper? What do you know to be true? What statement gives you a warm, energizing feeling, one that boosts you up and makes you feel whole? Counter your inner critic voice with a positive affirmation. Write it down here: *You are compassionate, eager to learn, and you are educated.*

Write as many positive affirmations as come to mind.

The list you are creating may be long or short, but with this list you are now equipped to show your inner critic voice the door as soon as it shows up wanting to beat you down. Tell it to take a hike, and let it know you no longer believe what it's saying. Tell it your positive affirmation(s), this decreases its power and increases yours. Remember, that's how you wake up the lion in you. You are stronger than you think you are! You can create a new you if you really want to!

It's not what you are that holds you back,
it's what you think you are not.
~Denis Waitley

CHAPTER 3

Harness the power of your mind

Even though I endured the hardships in Eastern Germany and a difficult transition to West Germany, my visualization about a better life came true. I met my "Prince Charming" when I was 18 years old on a kayaking trip in Southern France. I fell in love the moment I saw him. He unfortunately fell in love with one of the other girls in the group and did not notice me at all, no matter what I tried. I simply blended into the scenery. It was torture watching him attending to her all day long! I needed to get creative and make myself noticeable before the end of the trip, or I would most likely never see him again.

I threw caution to the wind and got in his face – literally, not worrying about rejection. After all I had nothing to lose, only to gain – possibly. I stole his shoe without him knowing while he was sitting at the campfire next to my competition the last day of the trip. I filled it with water, snuck up behind him and dumped it on his head, then ran for my life. It worked! Turns out, we got married six years later. I loved this man with all my heart, and he loved me the same. We had a "Cinderella" wedding like I had always envisioned. Before we married, we each lived with our parents. After getting married, we started a new life living together in our own apartment.

It all seemed perfect, but it wasn't.

We both ignored the fact he had an addiction to gambling. I knew about it before we got married, but I was young and in love, so I thought we could work through it together. Sadly, we were unable to deal with the elephant in the room. His gambling addiction created massive financial instability for us. I feared for our future as we both wanted to build a life together and have a family. I tried many different avenues—counseling, self-help groups, I participated in gambler's anonymous—all by myself to learn more about this addiction, but at the end I could not figure out how to help him and help us. It was devastating. I came to the realization that I couldn't change my husband, I could only support and encourage him. The change needs to come from the other side. My husband was not ready to change his ways at the time, so I had to make a choice—whether to stay or to leave.

I made a painful decision. I decided to leave…the man I loved so much. Our individual worlds shattered, and we both broke into pieces the day of our divorce!

This event took a huge emotional toll on me that threw me into a period of darkness. I found it very difficult at the time to maintain my positive outlook. I started to believe life would never change for me, and that I would continue to face one challenge after another. I started thinking I couldn't get things right, make a right decision, fix what needed to be fixed, and live a happy life. Things were not working out for me the way I had envisioned them. There were no roadblocks in the vision I had for my life, yet they seemed to appear all the time. *What the heck? Why me? What was I doing wrong?*

I could have dwelled on these draining beliefs about how things simply weren't going to work out for me and that I needed to accept this as the best life had to offer me. But those thoughts were devastating, and I wasn't ready to give up just because life continued to throw me one curveball after another. Instead, I made a conscious decision to believe there must be more out there and that a better life exists. Maybe not at the moment, but if I kept up my hope and pushed through the hard times, perhaps I would find my dream life one day.

My kick-ass "I can, and I will" statement resurfaced and helped me to keep moving forward. Not only that, I truly believe life is a God-given gift to each and every one of us. We can decide to treat life as a gift, making the best of each day with respect and gratitude, or we can choose to devalue it by living each day feeling sorry for ourselves and our life's circumstances.

Sadly, some people do that, they devalue their lives, day-in and day-out, but not me. That doesn't work for me.

I am happy and grateful to be alive. I hope and wish for you that you are grateful for your life and desire to make the best of it. Perhaps you feel stuck and don't know how to improve your situation, but as long as you have the desire to change your life for the better and are willing to work your way through the challenging times, you are on your way to living the best possible life you can imagine.

I was forced to start all over again when I found myself sitting in my new apartment heartbroken. My house of cards had collapsed, and I needed to get a new game plan together. I didn't have an idea how, but just making the decision to move on with my life helped me to see things from a new more positive perspective. So, it happened while riding the bus to work and reading the ads in the newspaper. I was looking for a used washing machine, but my "radar antenna" led my eyes to a different ad: "Come to beautiful Canada..." What? The ad sounded like a fantasy and too good to be true. However, my curiosity led me to pick up the phone and call the number that was listed in the ad.

The woman who answered the phone verified the ad was real. She told me that her brother, who had immigrated to Canada from Germany was building a house in Tofino, British Columbia, on the West Coast of Vancouver Island. He was looking for "guys" to help him build his house in return for free room and board. Since I was a woman, she wasn't sure her brother would entertain my offer to help him in return for a free stay, but she gave me his number so I could ask him myself. Little did I know that his number turned out to be my entry ticket into a whole new world. Perhaps you remember from Chapter 1, I dreamed about Canada as a child. Now I had found a way to turn this dream into reality.

With excitement and enthusiasm, I called the brother. He was reluctant at first, stating the job required help with laying shingles on the roof and putting drywall up, something I probably wouldn't feel comfortable with or know how to do. I admitted that I didn't know how to put up drywall or how to lay shingles on a roof, but just because I didn't know how didn't mean I couldn't learn.

I said, "I can, and I will try, and you can show me, right"?

How could he say no to that?

Thankfully, he said yes, which was a blessing to me. He must have liked my confidence and determination because I convinced him and he gave me the benefit of the doubt and said I could come at least for a trial. "Fair enough," I said, and so it happened. That same day I bought myself a ticket to Canada. What a difference a change in your outlook can make! It truly activates your "radar antenna."

Eleven years after East Germany, I still couldn't speak English, so I was a bit nervous about communicating halfway across the world in an English-speaking country, but what the heck? The guy I was going to work for knew how to speak German, and thus I did not dwell on that fact for too long. I had an anchor to hold on to, which felt sufficient. I also did not worry too much about not knowing how to do the stuff expected of me. If I had dwelled on this, I could have easily talked myself out of it. My inner critic threw all kinds of negative thoughts my way such as, *There's no way I can do this. I wish I could, but I can't. I don't have the knowledge or experience.*

But I did not let "the Grinch" take over. It was the opportunity that had gotten me excited, and my kick-ass power statement allowed me to focus on the possibility of success. I thought, *What do I have to lose? Worst case scenario I get booted, but what if I don't? What if it works out and I get to stay in the land of my dreams for a few weeks?* I liked those thoughts much better than *what if it does not work out.*

I ended up spending six weeks in Tofino and had the most amazing time. I loved it so much that I came back the following year for another six weeks. I also added on a two-week English crash course in Vancouver to learn the basics of the language because I was tired of always having to ask Franky to translate for me. I think it started to annoy him a bit as well, understandably.

On the plane home following my second year, I made a bold decision. I decided to make a move and start a new life in Canada, the land I had dreamed of as a child and that I had now fallen in love with. I had no idea how to pull it off, but I was going to find a way to make it happen. We'll get to that in the next chapter.

Some of my friends and clients alike often ask me, "How do you do it? How do you pull things off without having an idea how to do it? I wish I had the courage and would be able to just go with it, like you."

Let me share the ingredients of my secret sauce recipe on how I approach life in general, no matter how hard it sometimes seems, or when I don't have any idea of how to pull off the things I decide to do.

My Secret Sauce on How I Approach Life

#1 Follow your passion, do what's exciting.

#2 Focus on the possibility of success rather than failure.

#3 Never give up trying.

Winston Churchill once said, "**never give in**, **never give in**, **never**, **never**, **never**, **never**—in nothing, great or small, large or petty—**never give in…**"

That's it. That's the secret to my sauce. To sum it up, I'll share with you one of the most profound statements I've ever heard, shared by my friend JR, while at a yoga retreat, which encompasses all three of the above. **"Always follow your highest excitement keeping a positive mindset regardless of the outcome."** That is exactly what I do, I could not say it in a better way.

It doesn't always work out. Sometimes it gets me to amazing places, and other times I end up in a "construction zone." Those situations bring on new challenges that need to be dealt with when they occur. Is that always easy? No! To be honest, some choices I've made in the past pushed me down to the ground. They challenged me to my limits, but I always pulled myself out of the mess I was in with my empowering statement "I can, and I will." I learned from those challenges. You might know the saying, "What does not kill you makes you stronger." As blunt as it may sound, there is some truth to it, my friend. You grow from experiences, good or not so good.

Let's dive a little deeper into my secret sauce and how it works for me. The important thing is your mindset. That's where it starts. Keeping a positive attitude and not worrying about the outcome is crucial as this is what gets you emotionally involved and drives you to forward moving action. It enables you to make a decision and go with gusto, because the excitement you feel when moving forward in a positive way gets the juices in your body flowing and gets you moving. Your positive mindset lets you focus on the possibility of "what if it works out?" and diminishes the negative thoughts that creep up to discourage us like "what if it does not?"

When we think, "I can't do that, I can't do what I really want to do," because "I am too this or too that, things never work out for me," those negative thoughts trigger negative feelings, like "it's hopeless." Those feelings trigger our actions, or sometimes lack of action. Often, we can end up trying to talk ourselves out of things because we think it's useless anyway. Not trying ends up with unsatisfying results, and those reinforce the belief we had to begin with "I thought so, it didn't work out again." And so it becomes a recurring and frustrating battle. We worry, we doubt, we fear. As I mentioned before, fear is one of the greatest battles we all fight. It not only zaps our energy, but often completely paralyzes us and holds us back from truly living and being joyful. Whether it's fear of failure or fear of success, both resemble our struggles of leaving behind what's familiar to us because we fear the unknown.

It's easier to stay comfortable and stagnant than to step through the fog of fear, worrying whether we will find clear skies and sunshine on the other end or get completely lost in the fog. Either way, it's frightening, because we often don't know what to do next. What if we fail, what if we succeed? Will we be able to handle the outcome? Those are all understandable concerns!

Yet, we need to understand that what we want for our life is bigger and more important than fear, thus we must decide to overcome our fears and overhaul our belief systems. I truly believe facing our fears is the bridge between us and our greatest opportunities. The life we desire is on the other side of fear. Happiness, strength, love, courage, confidence, prosperity, peace, and all else you hope and dream of awaits on the other side.

Former First Lady Eleanor Roosevelt said it this way "You gain strength, courage and confidence by every experience in which you really stop to look fear in the face… You must do the thing you think you cannot do." The question is how can we do it? How can we look fear in the face? It's a question I've been asked a lot because I'm often perceived as fearless. Heck no, I am not fearless, but I've come to realize that fear is determined to conquer us if we are not determined to conquer it. If we don't put our protective gear on and find ways to overrule our fears, life will just happen around us and to us. That's not something I want to experience. What about you?

Quite honestly, fear will always be on our "list of feelings" as we will experience some level of fear for the rest of our lives no matter how strong we think we are. Every time we start something new, take on a challenge, or push our limits, we will encounter some sort of fear. The question is whether we let the fear hold us back from doing what we want or not. Here's good news though—we can win this battle; there is hope!

You see, we need to understand that it is our mindset we have to address if we truly want to change ourselves and our lives for the better. We need to understand that our thoughts trigger our emotions, our emotions trigger our actions, and our actions lead to the results, which in turn reinforces our belief system. It's a never-ending cycle that starts with our thoughts and beliefs. We need to understand that self-limiting beliefs are destructive and hold us back from what we ultimately want to have or achieve in our lives. Self-limiting beliefs, like "I can't do that, I don't know how, I am too weak, I am too old, I am too afraid" and so on, are draining. They suck the energy out of us. Those beliefs negatively shape our identity and the way in which we make decisions because they block us from stepping up and into our greater potential. On that note, let me share with you tool #3.

TOOL #3: Train Your Brain to Believe "I CAN, and I WILL"

We need to be aware of our thoughts and go to war with the thoughts and beliefs that don't serve us well. I believe we all are capable of winning this battle—that's what motivated me to write this book. I truly believe God gave each and every one of us unconquerable power to create and experience the life of our choosing. I am not saying it's easy, but it's possible. Every one of us has the potential for greatness, and yes, my dear friend, you do too! If you start to believe in yourself, you might be amazed what life has in store for you. Like the great Napoleon Hill once said, "Whatever the mind can conceive and believe, the mind can achieve."

Believing in yourself is a choice. It's an attitude you develop over time. It is your choice and your responsibility to take charge of your own self-concept and beliefs. Nobody can or will do that for you. You must decide. If you choose to believe that you can do anything you set your mind to, anything at all, even if roadblocks show up, you'll be surprised that you actually have it in you. You CAN! If you assume in favor of yourself and act as if it is possible, then YOU WILL do the things that are necessary to get results in your favor. If you believe it's not possible, you will not do what's necessary to produce results in your favor. Either way, it's another self-fulfilling prophecy.

I have never written a book, nor do I know how to write one. Just that fact alone could trigger self-limiting beliefs, and it did. One of the many questions I've been asked is, "What kind of a writer are you?" Ha, the first thought that came to mind was "I am not a writer at all, who am I kidding?" My next thought was "If I am a writer, I have no idea what kind," followed by "my English grammar sucks, and I don't really know how to write proper sentences." After all, English is my second language. Even though I attended the two-week crash course in Vancouver, the rest I learned by doing. I still make mistakes and pronounce words the wrong way, and I say things that don't make sense when translating a German thought to English. These are concerns that could have put doubts in my mind to prevent me from writing, but I chose to move forward with self-imposed confidence, reminding myself, "Who am I not that I could not tackle that challenge?"

Again, while negative thoughts surface, I don't focus on them and let them take control as they don't serve me well. My husband suggested that I study grammar to make myself more comfortable while writing. Yikes, that didn't sound like fun to me, and it didn't excite me at all. I did not like grammar in German, let alone English. What do we have editors for, huh? They correct what does not make sense, or does not flow, or needs fixing in any other way. So why would I bog myself down with all the flaws I have when it comes to the English language? It would just confirm that I indeed have these flaws rather than letting me explore what I am capable of despite the fact I am dealing with them.

I am who I am with my strengths and my weaknesses. English will always be my second language, and that's okay. So, I'll kick those doubting thoughts out the door and do what's exciting, keeping a positive mindset regardless of the outcome! Of course, I hope people will read my book, be inspired by it, take life changing actions and promote it to others, but I am open to whatever happens. I am learning so much along the way, if nothing else, it's a journey of self-discovery and so many aha moments…that alone is worth the effort.

It's often that I don't know how to do things, but the excitement gets me moving, and my "I can, and I will" attitude gives me the strength to figure things out as I go. When I trip and fall and end up in the ditch, I use the same attitude to pull myself out of the mess, no matter how bad it hurts. There is always a chance of getting bruised, regardless of what we do. But we can't let that risk stop us from trying and then throw in the towel if we don't succeed. We need to accept that failure is unavoidable and prepare ourselves to handle an outcome that is not in our favor. Shit happens, that's part of life. We need to embrace failure and choose to see it not as failure, per se, but as a learning opportunity. After all, we are going to learn something from the journey, wouldn't you agree? Besides that, without failure, how would we ever appreciate success? So, give yourself permission to fail and take the data as an opportunity to learn what works and what doesn't and keep going. That's the key! No matter how many failures you encounter, keep moving and maintain a positive mindset! Like an anonymous writer once wrote "Success consists of staggering from failure to failure without loss of enthusiasm."

One of my favorite quotes (not sure who wrote it) is: "Reach for the stars, spread your wings, and fly, you never know what you can do until you try." Doesn't that sound exciting? The possibilities are endless if we just try. So, how can we do it? How do we prepare ourselves to fight the battle of self-limiting beliefs and come out the winner?

The way to deal with the beliefs that don't serve you well is to acknowledge them. Tell yourself it's okay to doubt your capacity and to worry and experience fear. After all, we are human beings with feelings. Once acknowledged, we need to throw away those self-limiting beliefs that are holding us back from what we want to achieve in our lives and turn them into empowering beliefs that enable us to get the results we desire. It's like cleaning the house before we paint to give things a new and refreshing look. We've got to clean the dust and spider webs off the walls, otherwise we won't get the results we are happy with.

I can hear you saying "It all sounds great, but how do you kick those self-limiting beliefs out the door? I am not you; you seem to handle all things so well." Well, my friend. I seem to have a better handle on things today, but I had to learn it, sometimes the hard way. Today I am putting my knowledge to work for me, thus I am able to deal with challenges better. But in the past, I had my struggles as well when I let my fear and/or doubtful thoughts and emotions drive my actions or worse yet, lack of action. So, let's talk about how we can kick those self-limiting beliefs out the door.

PUTTING THIS TOOL INTO ACTION

Have you heard of Marie Kondo, a Japanese organizing consultant? Her KonMari Method™ of decluttering a messy home is intended to improve your happiness as well as your performance. Marie's *Life-Changing Magic of Tidying Up* explores how putting your space in order causes "correspondingly dramatic changes in lifestyle and perspective." Marie encourages people to get rid of items that no longer have a purpose or "no longer spark joy" and only keep items that are purposeful and meaningful. I have not organized my house in this way, but like that approach in general. We can do the same when addressing our mindset and throw away all the beliefs that don't serve us well or don't "spark joy" and keep the thoughts and beliefs that lift up and improve our happiness (as well as our performance). I love the quote from Marcus Aurelius: "The happiness of your life depends upon the quality of your thoughts: therefore, guard accordingly, and take care that you entertain no notions unsuitable to virtue and reasonable nature."

So, how can we guard our thoughts and beliefs and only keep those that "spark joy" and help us to attract the things we are missing to feel good, happy, and fulfilled?

Affirmations, as covered in the previous chapter, are great at helping to overcome the beliefs that don't serve us well, but there is more to it. We need to dig a little deeper to find out where these beliefs are coming from, how true they really are, and how they affect us. Finding answers to these questions will help us to modify our beliefs to make achieving goals easier. Beliefs are choices, subconsciously or consciously. The goal is to consciously drop the disempowering beliefs that are limiting our options and exchange them for empowering beliefs that help us to attract what we want to achieve in our life and/or who we want to become.

1. **Identify the beliefs that you think are limiting you.**
   For example:

   "I am never going to be in shape"
   "I'll never be able to buy the house I want"
   "I am not smart enough to...."
   "I am too weak to...."
   "I am not worthy"
   "I am not competent"
   "I am too afraid"
   "I can't do things right and always fail"

2. **Ask yourself, where do these beliefs come from?**
   Did you adopt a certain belief throughout your childhood or adulthood? Did it get reinforced in school, at work, from negative comments by others in your life, or through "failures" you experienced?

3. **Ask yourself, how true are these beliefs?**
   Is it really true that you'll never be in shape or not smart enough or capable enough? Perhaps you are not in the shape you want to be or somewhat limited in your ability to do certain things – at this moment in time – but does that mean you can't improve?

4. **Ask yourself, how do these beliefs affect you?**
   Are you happy with the life you have built for yourself and those around you? Are these beliefs ruling your life and stopping you from doing what you want to do?

5. **Think about how you would rather be, feel, or act.**
   Confident, emotionally strong, intelligent, thoughtful, financially stable, physically fit, etc.

6. **Now turn your limiting beliefs into empowering statements,** just like the affirmations we talked about in the previous chapter. Here are some examples:

   "I can and I will lose weight"
   "I will be able to buy that house one day"
   "I am smart and capable"
   "I am strong and able to...".
   "I am as deserving as all people on earth"
   "I am competent"
   "I am courageous"
   "I can do things right, and if I fail, I'll learn and grow from the experience"

Compare how you feel after reading each of your self-limiting beliefs versus your empowering beliefs. Does the belief make you feel good and spark joy within you? Do you want to sing and dance and get moving or does it make you sad and create hopelessness, like you don't even want to try?

By declaring war on your self-limiting beliefs and turning them into empowering beliefs that turn into positive affirmation, you allow your greater potential to start working for you. Think of the rotating cycle we've been talking about. Positive thoughts trigger positive emotions which trigger forward moving actions and create the possibility for great results. Again, I am not saying we are guaranteed success every time we choose to move forward, but we will stagnate if we don't try.

As I mentioned before, things don't change overnight. Daily practice is what it takes to develop skill, gain muscle, and perform better over time. You've got to **make an effort** each day to **train your brain** to believe **you can and will become** that high-performing athlete! So, out with the clutter that's holding you back! Think about all the possibilities ahead of you—and how your life will change for the better. Get excited about it and try it—a rule that has worked well for me.

**Here is your ACTION STEP for this tool.
Use it now!**

What self-limiting beliefs are taking up too much space in your mind? Put on your detective hat and think of all the thoughts and beliefs you are holding on to that don't "spark joy" and hold you back. Write them down on a piece of paper. Next go through the questions adapted from steps 2 – 5 listed above:

- Ask yourself, where do these limiting beliefs come from?
- Ask yourself, how true are these limiting beliefs?
- Ask yourself, how do these limiting beliefs affect you?
- Think about how you would rather be, feel, or act.

Now turn those limiting beliefs into empowering statements. Write those down on a separate piece of paper. Hang that paper somewhere where you can see it daily, then take the paper with the self-limiting beliefs, crumple it up, and throw it in the garbage! Remove the garbage from your house to make room for your greatness!

Believe you can and you're halfway there.
~Theodore Roosevelt

CHAPTER 4

Focus on the target no matter what gets in your way

As you now know, when I came back from my second trip to Canada, I made a bold decision to start a new life there. I liked the people and their relaxed lifestyle much more in comparison to the elbow-budging, me-first society I experienced in Germany. Things seemed to be more laid back in the Pacific Northwest, not so hectic and pushy. People wait their turn in Canada, while in Germany they would push their way through, flip the finger at you, or honk their horn if you weren't moving fast enough.

In Germany, things are written in stone. There is a long-lived tradition that is expected to be followed, "This is the way it is. This is how we do things." In the Pacific Northwest, things seem to run based on what makes sense. People treat you with more respect, like not cutting in line, which is commonly done in Germany. I fell in love with the kindness and compassion I found in the new world I discovered in North America. The culture is more focused on the "us" and the "we" rather than the "I" and the "me." Combined with the natural beauty of the Pacific Northwest, it became clear to me that this was the place I wanted to live my life moving forward.

I had no idea on how to pull it off, but I was going to find a way to make it happen. As exciting as the thought was, it was also a bit scary. *What am I thinking? That's crazy. I don't even know how to speak English well yet. Where would I live? What would I do to make a living? And how the heck would I immigrate to begin with?* All of those thoughts and more of the "hold back, that's nuts, you can't do that" beliefs surfaced. But this time, I overpowered those fearful thoughts with positive ones: *What if I can pull it off? What if I can make it happen? Holy smokes, how cool would that be?* My "I can, and I will" statement put a huge smile on my face. Just the possibility of it working out was enough to help get me moving in that direction.

Not knowing how this would all work, I started with the basics. The first step on my list was finding out how to immigrate to Canada. I did not have any family living in Canada who would sponsor me, so that avenue was not an option. I also didn't have a million dollars or whatever the amount is that's required to build a business and offer employment, which was another way people could buy themselves an entry ticket into Canada. The third option was to marry a stranger and go the green card route, just like in the movies. That thought turned my stomach upside down and was not an avenue I was going to explore. There was one other option left that was within my reach, working as a "Live-In Caregiver" for two years, after which time I could apply for permanent residency.

This meant climbing down the ladder from having a secure job as a social educator with benefits, vacation pay, living an independent life, and making good money, to living with and working for someone else in the same house as a servant. While that thought was not very appealing to me, it was the only way I would be able to make the move. So, I decided to do it. To overcome the rather depressing feeling that was associated with giving up my job to work more for less and more importantly giving up my independence, I told myself to focus on the end result of becoming a legal immigrant of Canada. "If that's what it takes, that's what I'll do."

So, I started to put my feelers out to find an available Live-In Caregiver job, and to my own surprise found one in only a few days through another newspaper ad. My "radar antenna" was working again for me. "German husband and Canadian wife with three small children are looking for a Nanny to take care of them and teach them German." Brilliant, I thought, what a great opportunity. I called right away and got the job, because of my training and experience working as a social educator. I was thrilled. If I would have been able to do a backflip, I would have done one. But that skill is way out of my league. With excitement and enthusiasm, I quit my job in Germany, canceled my lease agreement, sold my household belongings, and packed all that would fit into two suitcases. Canada, here I come. Remember my secret sauce on how I approach life? "Follow your highest excitement, keeping a positive mindset regardless of the outcome." While I had all the reasons in the world to talk myself out of what others considered crazy, I was thrilled about the opportunity and nothing or nobody could stop me from trying.

When I told my mother what I was doing, she handled it with grace, love, and compassion. She was not going to hold me back from something I wanted to do. She knew I would live with regret if I didn't take the chance. Even though my mother did not like me moving nearly five thousand miles away, she supported my decision while everyone else thought I had lost my marbles. Giving up all my securities, starting over in a new country with a foreign language I barely spoke, and climbing down the ladder to be a nanny? Not that there's anything wrong with being a nanny, it's just a different lifestyle working for someone in their house versus being independent, especially when you already earned a degree. My gosh, this is nuts!

"I could never do this" is what I heard from all directions. My friends and peers could not understand how someone could do such a bold thing because it's so scary. The fear of the unknown disabled their ability to comprehend what I was doing. I believe some of their lack of acceptance came from the same cultural pressures I was choosing to leave behind. This points out how some of our limiting beliefs are created by the society we live in, which was another reason why North America was then, and still is, so attractive to me. It's truly a land of opportunity.

While those fear-based thoughts popped into my head too, the opportunity to be able to start a new life in Canada excited me way more than worrying about all the details and whether it would work out in the end or not. I figured, *I can, and I will make this work and if it truly doesn't work out, I'll deal with it when the time comes.* And so it happened, I found myself back on a plane to Canada to start my new life there. Immigration was my first goal, everything else would come later. One thing I did then and still do miss about Germany besides my family and friends was the massive amount of vacation time I used to get, six weeks plus all the holidays! Yup, it was a really great job that I left.

As you may imagine, I was super excited to arrive in Canada. But oh boy, little did I know what waited for me at what I thought would be my new home for the next two years. I could write another book just about my life as a nanny that I would title the "Selfishs." The "Selfishs" were rich beyond any measure. I had never seen such a home. It was more of a palace full of splendor beyond what I'd seen in the movies. Inside were thirteen bathrooms, work and show kitchens, a gigantic home theater, two pools, luxury cars parked in the garage, to name a few of the splendors. Whoa! It was as fascinating as it was frightening. The movie *Cinderella* came to mind, I knew right away I was going to be a servant in this house, not a family member, like most Nannies are. I had to surrender my life to the woman I named "Miss Majesty," who thought she was made of gold and treated everyone around her like dirt. Again, back in a cage I thought. Shit, that's not what I had envisioned.

My life at the Selfishs was hard and pushed me to my limits every day. The way I was treated, especially by "her highness," who was my age for crying out loud, was utterly disrespectful. I am an ox and can take a lot of lumps, but that woman managed to bring me to tears every once in a while. She had no love or compassion for anyone and sadly not even her own children. I barely saw her, which was actually a blessing as it was difficult enough to have to deal with her orders and the comments she wrote in our "communication book" that lived on the kitchen counter. Then there was the intercom to which she would yell into. She often told me to not let the children know when she was home, or worse, she would call me on the intercom and order me to pull her kids away from outside her door when they knew she was in there and were asking to be let in.

So, I was glad our paths didn't cross too often. It was sad though for the children as they did not get to see their mother much either. Her agenda rarely included the kids, and then only on special occasions, where she would show them off like monkeys in the zoo. Other than that, there was no room for the kids in her or her husband's life. Even when they were home with the children in the room, they would order me to remove them. Mr. Selfish did not want to be bothered while watching his hockey games while Miss Majesty escaped to her bedroom suite doing whatever. This ordeal left me bathed in sweat every time as the kids rebelled, understandably. They wanted to be with their parents more than with me. What a mess, it made me so angry that parents could be so unloving toward their children. I was an adult and could manage their harsh treatment, but the kids did not understand why mommy and daddy were never available. *Why even have kids?* I thought, but that's their question to answer, not mine.

The days were long, and the nights were restless as Moritz and Bella, the three-year old twins, ended up sleeping with me in my twin bed and little two-year old Flynn cuddled in the housekeeper's twin bed down in the basement. This is while each of the kids had their own suite with a private bath, walk-in closet, and oversized custom-made children's beds. It was great for them to have so much room during the day, but at night the kids were frightened in their rooms. So it happened that most nights, the housekeeper and I had cute, sleepy, little kiddos coming to visit us on their tippy toes. She and I both got up sleep-deprived and exhausted most days, as we did not have it in us to send the kids back to their rooms. We felt tremendously sorry for them. They had everything a child could possibly want, yet not what they so desperately needed, the love and care of their parents.

My compassion for the kids helped me endure the challenges throughout the days as those snuggly and sweet little munchkins would turn into monsters at sunrise. The apple didn't fall far from the tree, if you know what I mean. Bella was a miniature version of her mom, and Moritz was angry at the world, which often turned into aggressive, rebellious behavior. Little Flynn had his moments too, and as cute as he was, he was a sly young dog.

Even though I felt sorry for the children and the way they had to grow up, I felt sorry for myself too. Each day was a new battle to fight. The kids did what they wanted and started screaming or biting if I requested anything of them that they did not feel like doing. I tried hard to apply all the educational knowledge and experience I'd gained back in Germany while going to college and working as a social educator, but those kids did not respond to any of it. It was frustrating, exhausting, and sometimes even humiliating. I still remember the day Moritz bit my hand while we performed the German "Edelweiss" song in front of all the kindergarten parents. As much as I excused the child's behavior because of his upbringing, it was tough on me and my spirit.

Besides that, I barely got a day off that I so desperately needed to rejuvenate. How could I leave on my days off when no parent was in sight to take care of the kids? So, I worked and worked and worked and fought back the best I could when Miss Majesty attacked me with her orders and verbal abuse or the kids tested my patience to the limits. I found it especially ridiculous when I was told how to raise the children and educate them. Seriously? That woman had no idea about education whatsoever, but mostly she lacked love and compassion. I had to bite my tongue often not to tell her a piece of my mind, because it was not my place to do that.

I felt like quitting more than once, packing up my stuff and flying home. Gosh, on those days I literally had to throw water in my face and remind myself what I was there for. Yes, to take care of the kids first and foremost, but the ultimate goal was to go through the Live-In Caregiver program so I could immigrate after serving my time. That was my goal. Honestly, I really did feel I was a captive in the Selfishs' house while counting the days until I satisfied the Live-In Caregiver requirements. In my wildest dreams I did not imagine it being so tough. I was tempted to tell the Selfishs to buzz off, words that I don't take lightly at all, but my goodness, they pushed my buttons all the time, parents and children alike.

It required my utmost focus and willpower to continue and not to give up (a part of my secret sauce, remember—to never give in). One of the things that helped me to pull through was when I met Wally in what little spare time I had through some friends I made down the street. He was German, handsome, and wealthy, which was not something I look for in a man, but it was a nice bonus. He flattered me and treated me like a princess in the few moments I could get away, which felt great after being treated like Cinderella all day long. He actually suggested I should leave the current situation I was in and work for his brother's family who could use a Live-In Caregiver. While that sounded very tempting, I didn't have it in my heart to abandon the little "monsters" under my care. If I had known then what I knew a few months later, I would have taken his offer. As the phrase "hindsight is always 20/20" indicates, it's easier to analyze and evaluate situations more clearly when looking back.

Here is what I learned after four months into the job. The Selfishs had no intention whatsoever of helping me with my immigration papers. They never applied for me as they agreed to, although they told me they had and that things were in the works. It took me a few months to realize that, but it eventually dawned on me that they were using me. Without the papers filed, I was not gaining any months toward the two years I needed for my immigration. Basically, I was a white slave living illegally in Canada. I fought through the days for what?

It was a rude awakening, but ultimately, I felt it was my fault because I trusted things would work out as they are supposed to. I was young and a bit naive. I trusted others to take care of things when they said they would without verifying they actually did. So, in the end, there was no one to blame but myself. I was shooting at the target with my eyes closed. That did not work very well. I missed it!

Failing forward, which means recognizing failure as a learning opportunity and moving on, I knew I had to find a different Live-In Caregiver position. I learned a tough lesson about paying more attention to the details and not trusting others unconditionally until they have earned that trust. Just because I value trust does not mean everyone else does, and it's important to understand that it can hurt or create conflict if you live with or work for someone who doesn't share similar values. I'll dive deeper into this matter in the next chapter.

My biggest conflict was having to decide in *my* favor instead of the kids'. But after all, it wasn't my job to take care of the kids until they grew up, yet I could not bring myself to leave. As monstrous as they were during the day, when they came to snuggle at night wanting to be cuddled and loved, the thought of not being there anymore for them was heartbreaking. How could I leave them in this awful situation without love and care? It took me four more months to make the decision in my favor and leave the kids behind. When the time came, I wrote a note in our "communication book," packed my bags, and left the next morning before anyone was awake. To this day, I don't regret sneaking out as I am certain Miss Majesty would have torn my head off and created a huge conflict within the household that would not have been healthy, neither for myself nor for the children.

I needed to get focused again on my goal. Some of my friends were saying "you wasted eight months?" and I'd say, "Yes and no, because I got to be the children's angel for a while, and that's not time wasted." I felt very blessed to have been able to be there for the kids and give them the love and care that they so desperately needed from their parents. I know it was not long enough, but I hope I was able to show them at least a sliver of what it feels like to be loved and cared for. Besides that, staying shaped me into a better version of myself and made me stronger, I learned how to persevere in the face of adversity.

Before this unfolded, I had met a German family with four children that was looking for help just down the hill from the Selfishs. We were a great match. I liked them, they liked me, and I spoke German, which was a plus because the parents wanted to raise their kids bilingual. Since my time at the Selfishs did not count toward my two-year requirement,

I had to start all over again. To make this work, I had to go back to Germany to await proper paperwork. Because I started out on the wrong foot at the Selfishs' house, I learned to pay more attention this time to verify the immigration program rules were followed to the letter.

Returning home, I spent time with family and friends, which was refreshing after eight months of slavery. When my official paperwork arrived, I flew back to Canada to repeat the whole process of immigration. Even though I was upset about the fact that I had lost all that time and had to start from scratch, I tried not to focus on that thought. It was water under the bridge and in the past, so I decided to focus on the future and move forward. I still had the same goal, I just missed it the first time. I can't blame anyone as I alone am responsible for not having approached it in a more diligent manner, paying more attention to the details.

Life with the German family was busy with four children, but we had a lot of fun together and enjoyed each other's company in a respectful and loving way. My plan was to finish the two years with them, but my world shattered again when Wally cheated on me. He had treated me like royalty and flew with me to Germany when I had to go back, just to be with me. When he had to return home for work, he bought me a ticket to Arizona so that we could spend Christmas together as I was not allowed to re-enter Canada without proper paperwork. He carried me on a golden plate, then dropped me like a hot potato, "not with intention" per his words.

Back in Canada, he had just thrown a huge party for me and my mom who had come to visit, when I caught him the next day in bed with someone else. He said, "It was not meant for your eyes." Really? I guess not! Little did I know that this was the way he lived his life as he explained later to me when he said, "It does not mean much, it's not serious. Those women are like ships, they come, visit the harbor for a day, and then leave." I was supposed to accept that? Holy shit, what a screwed-up mind.

He did not want to lose me, yet planned on living his life the way he pleased. I suffered tremendously from that discovery—another breach of trust that hit me even harder because it came from someone I cared about deeply. My heart and spirit were broken to the point that it was hard for me to peel myself out of bed every morning, not to mention showing up to work and doing my job well. The whole experience made me so sick that I literally lost my hair and had to wear a wig for a long time. What a mess. I did not have it in me to finish my time with the German family as they were now good friends with "my guy," and there were just too many memories there. Sadly, for all of us, I decided to find another job and finish up my program time in a more isolated area so that I could recover and put myself back together.

This did not impact our friendship though, for which I am very grateful. They understood my struggles and accepted me leaving the position. Just imagine if I would have switched positions from the Selfishs to Wally's brother's home. Oh my gosh, what a mess that would have been. I am glad I stuck with my gut at the time.

What a way to immigrate, huh? This is not what I had in mind when making the move from Germany to Canada. I was not happy having to go through the Live-In Caregiver program to begin with, but it was the only way for me to gain entry. I worked to exhaustion, struggled through challenging days, and suffered through the emotional drama of being betrayed by the man I was in a relationship with. There were days when I asked myself if it's all worth it? I had a pretty good life in Germany, a good job, my own apartment, I made good money, and I was surrounded by family and friends. Yet, the answer was always "yes, yes, yes, it's worth it."

I believe in the "pot of gold at the end of the rainbow," and by that I don't mean monetary wealth. For me it was the fulfillment of my hopes and dreams living happily in Canada and being able to do what I wanted to do, just as I had envisioned it as a child back in East Germany. Nobody said it would be easy to get there, but I knew it was possible, and that's what I chose to focus on, no matter what hit me along the way.

It takes focus, willpower, and perseverance to go from where you are now to where you want to be. You might hit a few roadblocks or fail a few times, just as I did. No matter if you pursue a small or a big goal, you usually don't hit the bullseye the first time you shoot the arrow, unless of course you are a pro. But even pros miss every so often. The important thing is to not give up trying and to do what it takes— all the time. If you keep your eyes on the target and keep shooting arrows, you have a much better chance of hitting the bullseye one day. If you give up and stop trying because it seems too hard, your ego gets bruised, you fail too many times, or something takes the wind out of your sails, then all you will do is watch the days go by. You go through the motions of life and just keep on wishing things will change for you one day. Worse, you may get upset watching someone else hit the bullseye because they never stopped trying. Just think about Benjamin Franklin's profound statement for a moment: "An opportunity is never lost, it's simply found by someone else."

I love this statement because it holds the possibility for each and every one of us. It's saying if you don't go for the opportunity, someone else will, thus it implies that you could if you wanted to. It comes down to believing you can indeed get what you want. It comes down to decision-making. We covered "limiting beliefs" and how to conquer them in the last two chapters. Further, you need to fight the human tendency to take the easy and most comfortable route and choose to do what it takes to hit the bullseye! Willpower comes first. That is something nobody can take from you.

It's up to you whether you want to keep going with the flow, like floating down the river, or if you want to change your direction, swim upstream, or across the river against the strength of the fast-moving current. Swimming against the current is hard, but it's doable for each and every one of us. Of course, this is the harder route and requires consistent willpower and perseverance, but if continuing to do what you have been doing so far has not gotten you to where you want to be, perhaps you need to re-think your approach. We can train to build perseverance. The first step though is making the choice to change direction and that choice, again, is up to you. The amazing life you want, my friend, is not going to fall into your lap...at least not for most of us. Most of us have to work hard and stay focused to get what we want, no matter what hits us along the way.

You might think, "I am too weak, I don't have it in me to swim upstream. I tried a few times and nearly drowned every time; I simply can't do it." It's understandable that you think and feel this way, especially if you've tried before and failed. Yes, the upstream way is hard, but it carries possibilities. Isn't it at least worth trying? Once you make that decision in your favor, you can train your body and mind to become more persistent, so you are able to keep swimming against the current no matter how strong it is. Remember, "What you focus on expands!" and "Whatever the mind can conceive and believe, the mind can achieve."

It takes time and training to become a great and strong swimmer. How do athletes do it? They set time aside each day to train their body and mind to work hard to become stronger and improve their endurance to achieve their goals. Successful people are much the same, they develop a daily routine to maintain focus on the fulfillment of their goals. We need to do something similar if we want to change our lives for the better. We need to be proactive and do what it takes to stay focused and work toward our goals. Why not learn from achievers? They must be doing something right. I am thinking if they can do it, why can't you and me? What do you think?

While you can condition your body and mind to become stronger at any time in the day, I find it crucial to start first thing in the morning as it sets the tone for how you go about your day. If you get up thinking, "It's just another day to get through," it's likely you might drag your feet all day without accomplishing much of anything. Getting up in the morning with focus and determination by working through an empowering morning routine not only helps you become physically and mentally stronger, but it also helps you attract extraordinary things.

During those challenging days that I described earlier in this chapter, I got up every morning and no matter how exhausted or frustrated I felt, I focused on the good things in life rather than all the negative things that bombarded me right, front, and center. Thinking of things to be grateful for every day helped me to work through the challenging days. After all, I was in Canada. I enjoyed the kids snuggling with me, I had the housekeeper as a companion, and I could go to the gym every once in a while, so there were always things to be grateful for. Thinking of those things made me feel good and helped me to approach each day with a positive mindset.

Next, I would lay out the day ahead in my mind and think of something positive that would make the day special. Even little things, like no fighting at the breakfast table, for the kids to get in the car without screaming and yelling, or for me to have more patience and be especially loving. It always amazed me how much power those positive thoughts had. They not only put a smile on my face and helped me to look forward to the day, but there was also the possibility that it actually could happen. *So why not believe that it can?* I thought. Those thoughts fueled me with energy and strength to face each new day. I would finish the morning with a positive affirmation, like "I am loving, caring, and understanding," and then go tackle the day. That little routine was powerful for me and helped me stay focused on my ultimate goal, which was immigration and to be the best I could be throughout the day.

Today, I have a whole morning routine to start each day in a powerful way so I can stay focused and motivated to achieve my goals. I have a journaling book I use to write my thoughts down because I believe it's more powerful to actually put things on paper than to just think about them. I can also refer back to it later, which can often be very enlightening! As good as we like to think our memories are, the written word is forever. Having said that, let me share with you tool #4 and why I believe it will help you keep your eyes on your goals no matter what gets in your way.

TOOL #4: Power Up Your Morning Routine

Instead of getting up and just going about your day the way you are used to, you can "spice up" your morning routine to strengthen your physical and mental well-being. This will help you gain clarity on what it is you want to attract into your life and increase the level of commitment toward your dreams and goals. I know of a few people who drink red bull first thing in the morning to get energized. Hmm… not sure about that one to be honest. I guarantee you'll get more out of developing and practicing a daily empowering morning routine that will fuel you better than an energy drink.

I always **start my day with Gratitude.** I believe that gratitude is the key element to joyful living, it's a feeling that nurtures the soul. It's amazing how much gratitude can enhance your enthusiasm for life and the energy you bring to it. When you get up in the morning with gratitude, you recognize that each day brings new opportunities. That's uplifting and exciting, and lets you start the day with gusto. I believe there is always something to be grateful for if you allow your mind to be open to it. Even on days when I am really down and that "feeling sorry for myself" thought creeps up, I think of something to be grateful for. I focus on what's great in my life. It can be as simple as my morning coffee, a raindrop I see on a flower outside, or sometimes it's the sheer privilege of being alive that gets me going again. William Arthur Ward says this about gratitude: "Gratitude can transform common days into thanksgiving, turn routine jobs into joy, and change ordinary opportunities into blessings." Gratitude can have a positive snowball effect in your daily life, especially in tough or challenging situations. It can help you to manage yourself and others in a more respectful and loving way, which surprisingly can lead to others treating you the same way, too.

Next, I **think of one to three things** *I can do* **that would make today special or awesome** if achieved. I write those things down in my journaling book. I love this approach; it really gets me thinking with intention how I want to go about my day. Sometimes my thoughts are goal oriented and other times they have to do with something I would love to do, but usually don't have enough time for. While I always strive to achieve my goals or make time for things that are simple pleasures, I also strive to better myself and become the best I can possibly be. Therefore, I include self-improvement thoughts in my daily journaling, like "being a better listener today" or "being especially kind to others." And on those days when my mind is blank and I can't think of anything, I simply write "Life is good, let's be awesome today" in my journal. That always gets my juices flowing!

Once I write my thoughts or goals down for the day, I **create my Positive Affirmation.** We already talked about the effects of your self-talk and the dramatic influence it can have on your level of success in every aspect of your life. My positive affirmation usually supports one of the goals that I am writing down for the day. If I want to "get my to do list done" for example, my affirmation could be "I am determined, disciplined, focused, and action driven to get my stuff done."

When I am working on something very specific and need some extra help, like a kick in the ass so to speak, I go online and **search for a short video or podcast with a positive empowering message**. It can be motivational, spiritual, or educational. There are also short to-the-point mentoring programs you can sign up for that arrive in your email inbox daily or weekly. You could also **read a book that inspires you** and gets you moving. Whatever method you choose, I find this to be a powerful add-on. I believe that learning from others who have achieved a level of success is very inspiring and motivating and can help us when we feel stuck or discouraged. Look for things that are short and to the point that you can easily fit into your schedule. One word of caution though, as you search for speakers you like, watch the clock. Five minutes can turn into an hour quickly if you don't pay attention and get sucked in, especially when watching videos or listening to podcasts. It happened to me in the past and still does every once in a while.

I also strive to **include some exercise into my morning routine** as staying physically fit is super important for my overall well-being and mental state. I love Pilates, it's a low impact exercise on my body, yet it helps me build strength and keeps me in shape—if I do it daily. It's easy to fall off the wagon and skip the exercise part. I can name a few excuses, but truly, I feel much better if I make time for it. It's just another way of getting energized for the day.

Depending on how I feel, I'll **add a few minutes of meditation after the exercise part.** Practicing meditation is fairly new to me. I learned about the benefits of it at a yoga retreat I attended in 2018. While there are many different meditation techniques, at the end it's really just sitting still, in silence with or without your eyes closed, paying attention to your breathing, and learning to observe your thoughts and feelings without judgment. You can add meditation music and chant mantras. If you are not familiar with meditation and/or mantras, you can research it on the internet or join a class that offers it.

There's also a free app called "Insight Timer" that offers meditation for every topic or interest. The benefits to meditation are plentiful. It's like taking a magic pill that reduces stress, controls anxiety, enhances self-awareness and the body's immune system, helps control your thoughts, increases blood flow and slows the heart rate, and so much more. Many people in all walks of life, including known celebrities, CEOs, and other successful people use meditation regularly. I encourage you to give it a try and discover how it can be beneficial to you. You can do it just for just a few minutes or as long as you wish. Even a few minutes will give you benefits!

And here's a bonus for those who really want to up it and gain stamina: **Have a cold shower**! Yup, I know it's a tough one, but it really wakes up your body and your mind and gets your juices flowing. It's another "tool" I was introduced to in one of the yoga weekend retreats. Let me be honest, I had to force myself into doing it. I love hot showers…long hot showers. But believe it or not, you'll get used to the cold ones, plus there are health benefits on top of it! Researchers have found that cold water showers and/or plunges help improve your general well-being, increase your metabolism, improve circulation, help fight off common illnesses like colds and the flu, and even help relieve symptoms of depression as they jolt your system to increase alertness, clarity, and energy levels. Isn't that worth it?

PUTTING THIS TOOL INTO ACTION

Practicing a morning routine not only makes you feel good about yourself and life, it also assists you in taking any area of your life to the next level. But you've got to prioritize time for it. Otherwise, you might not do it. It comes back to choices and decision making. Where there is a will, there's a way! Perhaps you have to get up twenty minutes earlier than you normally do, but if that's what it takes, then it's up to you to decide to do so. Even ten minutes will benefit you! Yes, it can be easier at times to sit there and to not follow through, come up with an excuse or feel sorry for yourself because doing what's uncomfortable (like getting up twenty minutes earlier than normal) costs you energy and sometimes you simply run out of it. It's like a car without gas. You've run out of steam. It happens. We are human beings with strengths and weaknesses. However, we need to understand that without fuel, all we can do is push the car. If you've ever had to do it, you know how hard it is. Setting time aside to gain and maintain mental and physical strength is like fueling up at the gas station. If we don't "fuel up" frequently, we just push ourselves throughout the day, and nothing likely will ever change. That can be exhausting, frustrating, and about as exciting as watching paint dry.

I can only speak for myself here, but I can attest out of experience that if I don't practice my daily morning routine, it's much harder to stay focused and power through challenges. It can be easy to fall back to old behaviors that don't serve me well, like drinking an extra glass of wine in the evening and munching on too much cheese. Before I know it, I've gained a few pounds!

If you can relate to that, I encourage you to find the extra time to power up your morning routine. Think of it as drinking a booster shot in the morning. No, not red bull or tequila, I don't think those shots will get you the results you desire. I am talking about an "energy booster shot" with a bit of everything in it that's healthy for you and your well-being.

Here is a quick recap of some of the "booster ingredients" you can implement that can be a big game changer for you:

- Gratitude
- Ways In Which I Can Be Awesome Today
- Positive Affirmation
- Research
- Exercise
- Meditation
- Cold Shower

You don't have to include all the ingredients in your "drink," simply choose what works for you! It's all about conditioning yourself to get stronger mentally and physically so that you can stay focused on the achievement of your goals.

At the end of the day before going to bed, I find it very powerful to review the day and think of the amazing things that happened. I also think about **"Where could I have made a better choice today?"** which is also super powerful as sometimes we fall short of the things we want to do or bring into our lives. It's a great way to recognize the shortcomings we have, acknowledge them, and then try to do better the next day.

If we truly want to improve our lives, no matter in which areas, we need to **Keep our eyes on the target at all times,** because "Obstacles are those frightful things you see when you take your eyes off the goal," a statement Henry Fonda once made.

We also need to know why we are doing what we are doing. Why we are pursuing the goals we set out to achieve. That's equally important. **Your WHY matters**. It's a fuel enhancer for your gas tank, so to speak. Your why is your purpose. The dictionary describes purpose as "the reason for which something is done or created or for which something exists." You can see, there are two components to purpose—one for why something is done or created, which refers to our doing, the other for why something exists, which refers to our being. Both are equally important because defining your purpose for both will contribute to your overall happiness in life.

So, when you decide to change direction and swim upstream in an effort to change your life for the better, think about why you are doing it? Your WHY is what moves, drives, and energizes you and it helps you to get back up when you get knocked down or feel discouraged. Your WHY gives meaning to what you do. Without meaning, it's difficult to stay focused and motivated. If you don't know your WHY, it's easy to wander and drift, get sidetracked or quit what you started.

As I shared with you earlier, I had to deal with quite a few challenges at the Selfishs' house and more than once thought of packing up and quitting. Especially in those moments, my WHY helped me to stay focused on my goal and push through the hard times. I knew I wanted to live in Canada. This was my WHY and it kept me going when the going got tough.

Here is my last tidbit for this chapter. If you fall off the wagon once in a while and don't practice your daily morning routine, don't beat yourself up. Welcome to the club of human beings. Just hop back on the wagon and don't let self-limiting beliefs like "I don't have enough willpower" or "I am too weak" stop you from doing what gets you better results in your life. All that matters is that you never take your eyes off the target and keep shooting arrows toward the bullseye, so that YOU CAN one day hit it right in the middle!

Here is your ACTION STEP for this tool.
Use it now!

To get from where you are to where you want to be, you've got to push yourself beyond where you've been and what you've done, and you've got to do what's hard and push past it. That's uncomfortable. With that, my exercise suggestion for you is to get comfortable with being uncomfortable. Growth requires a constant state of discomfort. It's not something I claim to be an expert in, but many self-help books drive home that point. If you want to grow and better your life, I suggest getting used to being uncomfortable.

How?

Take a cold shower each morning. If I can do it, you can. The ideal way to take a cold shower is to ease into the habit. Start by slowly lowering the temperature at the end of your usual shower. Get the water cold enough that you start to feel uncomfortable. Then, stay underneath the water for two or three minutes. Breathing deeply will help decrease your discomfort in your mind. Also, watch your attitude. If you approach it thinking this is going to feel horrible, then that negativity will make it harder on you. Think about the health benefit and remind yourself that it is a way for you to get mentally stronger.

Here is another thought: Most people are unwilling to do what's uncomfortable because it's hard. However, those that push through are more likely to succeed in whatever it is they want to achieve than those who don't try or give up. I know cold showers are a shocking event, they are frankly unpleasant, but they truly boost your energy and strengthen your mental and physical well-being. That's well worth it to me. I hope and wish that it's worthwhile for you, too. By the way, cold showers help you to keep your eyes open, so you have a better chance of hitting your target.

Whenever you want to achieve something, keep your eyes open,
concentrate and make sure you know exactly what it is you want.
No one can hit their target with their eyes closed.
~Paulo Coelho

CHAPTER 5

Align yourself with your values

So, here I was halfway through this big adventure of immigrating to Canada finding myself struggling to finish my Live-In Caregiver time while dealing with the emotional drama of being cheated on by the man that had carried me on a golden plate. I felt like I'd gotten hit twice on my road to immigration. First by the Selfishs and their rude and reckless behavior and then by Wally, who wanted to "visit other ships in the harbor" besides me. I knew the immigration path wasn't going to be easy, but I did not anticipate these types of roadblocks.

As hard as it was, I was not going to quit, my WHY kept me going. I wanted to live in Canada, and I needed to find another job to finish up my time as a Live-In Caregiver, at which time I would be able to apply for permanent residence status. I had about a year to go. There was a light at the end of the tunnel.

Luckily, I found a new job fairly quickly. My "radar antenna" was working for me again helping me find what I needed to move on. It was a single father living on a small farm with horses, in need of help caring for his teenage daughter. That sounded intriguing to me; thus, I took the job. We got along perfectly fine and enjoyed each other's company. There wasn't too much for me to do there as he went to work all day, the kid went to school, and I just needed to take care of a few household things and cook dinner. When he came home from work, he went to his barn, put some country music on, opened himself a beer, and asked me to come and join him to hang out. Often, we ended up dancing to Shania Twain or any of the other upbeat country songs. This was a lot of fun, but the relationship was strictly platonic. Romance was not entering my life at this point. I had an amazing time there and really appreciated his generosity. He made a vegetable garden for me and let me ride one of his horses every day. I loved it, and I had time to put myself back together after the emotional drama I had been through previously. While I was spiritually recovering, my body was a bit slow to follow as I still needed to wear a wig.

On Sundays, I went to church, where the lady who always sat behind me said she knew someone I should meet. It was a widower with two small children. His wife had passed away from melanoma, and he had just moved a few months ago from the U.S. to Canada to be closer to his family. The lady was adamant about my meeting him, thus I had to listen to the same thing every Sunday. She did not let it go, even though I told her I was not interested in meeting anyone to go out with and certainly not a guy with two children. I just wanted to finish my time as a Live-In Caregiver and then move on with my life, not get bogged down with another relationship, especially not one that included two kids.

The lady owned a coffee shop where the dad would stop by every morning to pick up a cup of coffee and read the paper after going to the gym. She thought it would be the perfect place for us to meet. I should just be there at the same time and "bang," she thought we would fall in love. The only way for me to get her to stop nagging was for me to go meet the guy and get it over with. After months of her pestering, I was at the coffee shop "just by accident" at the same time he came there to drink his coffee. To protect his privacy as well as his name in the business world, I will call him "Sam." It wasn't love at first sight, like the "bang" the lady anticipated, but I have to admit I felt a spark and something in me started to shift, which made me go back to the coffee shop again and again.

Fast-forward a couple of months, as you may have guessed, we ended up in a relationship, against my initial reservations. We discussed the possibility of me finishing my two-year Live-In Caregiver program with him and his children to see how we would all get along. Besides that, Sam could use the help as he was going through nannies like they were out of style. "They all leave because the kids are so difficult," he said, and I thought it couldn't be that bad. It's understandable that they are troubled kids, having lost their mom at such a young age. And it's certainly not helpful that all the caretakers are leaving shortly after they have entered the children's lives. No wonder they are a bit of a mess.

I felt this would be fixable over time with love, compassion, understanding, and the consistency I believe is needed in a family. *I can bring that to the table*, I thought. We decided to move forward with that option. There was an extra suite in his house, so the setup was perfect, and I moved in. Also, in my mind was the possibility of adding on to the family when the time was right, even though Sam stated early on that he did not want any more kids. I felt he was overwhelmed at the time, so no wonder he would not want any more children. But let us all be together for a while, I thought, and things might look different.

The move was very difficult for my farm guy and his daughter as they did not want to lose me. I did not understand how attached they had become. He got so mad, he threw chairs through the room when I told him I was leaving, and the daughter went into my room and took scissors to all my treasured memory photos I had brought with me from Germany. Ouch, that hurt a lot and truly upset me, but I tried to understand their frustration. It wasn't my intent to cause them any pain. My time was almost up, so I would have left soon anyway. But I believe that in their minds, they thought I was going to stay with them forever and live happily ever after. My vision of the future was different, and I thought I had made it clear that once my time was up, I'd move on. Yet they seemed to hope that I would change my mind over time. It was another dramatic exit for me, one that I didn't see coming. It saddened me deeply that we parted this way as I was hoping we could stay friends, just as I am still friends with the German family.

Living with Sam and his children was a new "balancing act" that I had to perform on a daily basis. The kids were indeed very challenging and pushed me to my wit's end every day, like the Selfishs' kids had done. I tried to handle it the best I could, but it was frustrating and emotionally draining. We did not get along as I had hoped, yet I felt they did not rebel toward me as much as they rebelled at the world. They were both hugely impacted by the loss of their mother, and neither I nor anyone else seemed to be able to fill that void at the time. I still believed I was the right person to care for the children and that over time things would work out in favor for all of us. Let me explain why I thought I was in the right place, because my belief impacted the biggest and hardest decision I made in my life.

I came to find out that Sam's wife died the same day and year I was on a plane on my way to Canada to start a new life. That day, that year, Thanksgiving Day 1996. What are the chances? My ending up on the farm far away from where I started my two-year program, going to church, and sitting in front of the lady every Sunday who was so adamant about my meeting the single dad with two kids. All these things led me to believe the Lord had put me there. It was meant to be. With these thoughts in my mind, I believed I was the right person to take over the care of the children. However, I struggled with that thought, because it meant giving up my wish and desire to have my own children one day. Sam did not change his mind and made it pretty clear he was not going to have any more children. He did not want to bring a third child into the mix. That was the verdict. "Accept it or not, but that's it for me" he said.

I had to make a choice, again! Do I leave, or do I stay? I prayed a lot about it and always ended up with the same answer, "This is what you are meant to do, be their mama." I felt like running away from what became clear to me was my divine mission, just like Jonah, whose story is described in the Old Testament of *The Holy Bible*. He was called by God to be a prophet, but refused to accept his mission and left on a sea voyage instead. That sounded pretty good to me, leave on a sea voyage or any type of voyage for that matter as long as I did not have to do what was put in front of me. I wanted my own kids, and staying meant having to give up my dream of having them. That was a lot to ask of me! *Why me, why always me?* went through my mind.

If you happen to know Jonah's story, you know God caught up with him and his trip did not end well as he was swallowed by a whale, so it occurred to me that running away may not be the solution here. The thought of leaving also conflicted with my core values and general purpose in life, which is helping others and honoring the Lord with all my heart. I decided to stay and raise Sam's children, because I truly believed I was meant to be their mom. It was the hardest decision I have made to this day and also the toughest job in my life, because the kids were so challenging. Imagine landing a job in the tiger cage of the zoo. That's what it felt like to me because they were indeed little tigers at the time.

Sam and I got married four years after we met at the coffee shop. The kids, without my asking or telling them what to call me, instantly called me "mom" the day of our wedding. It was as if they were waiting for the day to come. Before they had simply called me by my name. I looked up to God and smiled as this seemed to be a confirmation of my "divine mission." Life continued to be challenging for us, as the kids continued to be little tigers and fought a lot with us and each other. I heard it's normal and happens in many families. Even though it was hard on me and my soul, I accepted our "zoo life" as normal, hoping that one day we would all get along like cuddling teddy bears.

When Sam and I got together, he did not work so he could take care of the kids. He had the financial means to do this. After about a year with me in the house helping with the kids and us just goofing off and having a good time, he decided to start working again in his field of business. He was a very successful real estate broker and developer. In the past, his deceased wife had worked with him, and we discussed the possibility of my replacing her in that role. The thought of us working together and me learning from the master was very appealing to me, plus I welcomed a change of pace.

Sam wanted to work in the U.S. again, thus we decided to move across the border to Bellingham, Washington. While Sam and the kids moved over the summer so the children could start the new school year in the U.S., I stayed in Canada for another few weeks to await my immigration ceremony to become a Canadian citizen. After completing the Live-In Caregiver program, I had become a permanent resident, which was a very proud moment in my life. Now sufficient time had passed, and I could apply to become a citizen, which I was not going to miss just because we were moving to Bellingham. I had made it, my dream of being able to live in Canada had come true. Now, a new opportunity presented itself, moving to the U.S., which was very exciting for me. This time, I had a husband on my side through whom I would gain immigration status, which was a welcome change! Besides that, we had the means to hire a lawyer who took over all the work and made the process go smoothly.

As much as I was excited about the opportunity to become a dual citizen, I was equally excited about working with Sam in the real estate industry and even more so when we decided to build a real estate team. Sam was a loner. Besides me and work, he did not welcome anyone else in his life, so we had no friends or close business associates. It did not bother him, but it troubled me, as I am a social butterfly and have always surrounded myself with friends. I value friends and friendship tremendously. Over time I started to feel an emptiness, because I had no one else in my life but him and the kids. So, I welcomed the idea of building a team. It meant I would have other people in my life again. We started out great, I got my real estate broker license, we signed up for mastermind coaching to learn the ins and outs about building a team, then implemented quickly what we had learned. Our team grew quickly to ten members, and our agents became successful in just a few months because they were taught by the master in the business.

While my workload increased substantially and consumed every free minute of my time, it was not the hard work that troubled me. Everyone who knows me can attest I am a work horse and can plow through the fields, no matter how hard the ground is. It was something else that started to nag on me, which took me some time to recognize. Sam had done business a certain way, which worked for him, where service providers did exactly what he told them to do because that was their job for which they got paid. This uncompromising approach does not work well amongst your own team. When it's your team, your employees thrive more with patience, tolerance, understanding, and the like. Sam's management style lacked those personal touches, thus we experienced conflict in our team. It wasn't on purpose or with malice, it was simply Sam's "my way or the highway" approach that did not sit well with the others. Even though I tried to be a buffer between Sam and each team member, it happened that slowly but surely, everyone chose "the highway." They wanted to feel like part of a family and not just a working machine. It was frustrating to see our team fall apart, but I could understand why those that left wanted to leave. With these work challenges and the stress we had at home with the children, life became more and more challenging for me.

And then there was more that added to my struggles. Sam started complaining about my looks, my weight, my hair, and the way I dressed. I hadn't gained any weight nor did my hair look like a mop, but I was always exhausted and tired. Perhaps that showed. I did my best, but my best was simply not good enough anymore. I do not believe he criticized me on purpose, as I came to discover the true hurdle in our relationship. It was the same issue that caused our team to fall to pieces. We had different core values. I had never given much thought to the values that are important to me, in other words, the standards or principles I chose to live by. I simply lived by them, they existed somewhere inside of me, but I had never really defined them.

It finally dawned on me that Sam's purpose in life was completely different than mine. Consequently, our core values did not match, which was the primary cause of the stress and conflict in our relationship. We had different internal beliefs on how to live life and how to go about things, from doing business to leading our personal lives. Because our values did not match, our actions and behaviors were not aligned, and conflict arose. It never really occurred to me how your values influence your behavior and attitude and ultimately contribute to the overall satisfaction of your life. This was an "aha moment" for me.

While my core values are mainly driven by the needs of others, Sam's are mostly driven by self-interest and personal achievement. I believe everyone has some self-interest as it's a natural survival instinct and necessary for personal growth. I would actually hope that you are reading this book with self-interest and a desire to increase your personal level of achievement. However, when another person's self-interest is coupled with a dominant personality type, it can be difficult to deal with when you value sharing and the well-being of others. The lifestyle benefits I had with Sam were nice, but not equal to the emotional cost I realized when compromising my values.

This goes to another aspect of relationships, the four different primary personality types that exist in humans, as described in the "DISC" profile. The profile describes human behaviors in various situations, how you influence others, respond to challenges, and rules and procedures. "D" stands for "Dominance" and is associated with a strong willed and forceful personality type. "I" stands for "Influence" and describes people who are sociable, talkative, and lively. "S" stands for "Steadiness" and classifies people who are gentle and accommodating, and "C" describes people who are "Conscientious," analytical, and logical. (Visit https://www.discprofile.com/what-is-disc/overview/ to learn more.) We all have a combination of the four personality types, but typically one stands out as primary. Sam is a "D" off the Richter scale. I am a "High I." I also have "D" in me, but way less compared to Sam, which lowers my need to win. Most times I ended up letting him win in our discussions and arguments because he was willing to escalate to a higher level than I was. Consequently, I would do things his way not only to keep the peace, but because I didn't have the same inherent drive to win as Sam. The unfortunate consequence of my doing this was that I compromised some of my values, which led to an internal emotional conflict I could not resolve.

This personal conflict made it impossible for me to stay in a happy and harmonious relationship with Sam. There was no hope of fixing things, because you can't change a person or their values or principles.

And if you compromise your values for anyone or anything, you run the danger of destroying your inner self, a message my mother taught me back in East Germany; it just did not click with me at the time. Sadly, that is what happened to me in my 30's.

My inner world shattered because I constantly compromised my core values. I felt my own personal integrity was being destroyed. I was turning into a puppet, just functioning day-in and day-out. The fire within me had burned out. It wasn't me anymore that existed, just a shell that became more brittle with the passing of time. We were in year four of our marriage. When I looked in the mirror, I saw someone else—not the funny, exciting, adventurous full-of-life Kerstin, but a squeezed-out lemon that had no juice left inside. The lion in me had gotten weaker over time from fighting battles every day and finally crashed from exhaustion. I had accepted the way things were and was just going with the flow to keep the peace. It made me sad though. I was not even 40 years old, but nearly felt dead inside. My life wasn't turning out the way I wanted it to. The world started to look gray again, just like it did growing up in East Germany.

I could not go on like that. Another divorce? I struggled with my first one, and the thought of getting divorced again stabbed me like a knife, but I did not see a different solution. Staying would mean to keep compromising my values and live unhappily ever after. That's not what I had in mind for my life. As weak as I felt and as much as I struggled with the thought of getting divorced, I made the decision to do whatever was necessary to get myself back together, which meant leaving and starting over, again! I wasn't going to give up and stay because at the time that seemed easier. After all, we lived a financially stable and comfortable life. But I discovered that the saying "all the money in the world can't buy you happiness" is true. I literally had no idea how to move on, and I was scared and afraid of making the move. *How many times does someone need to fall on their face before hitting the jackpot?* I thought, *Why me again? It's utterly brutal and not fair. Will things ever change for me or do I always seem to make the "wrong" choices?*

I came to the conclusion that our marriage was not the "wrong" choice at the time, but it was just not working anymore. I did not want to continue the way we were living and working together. The kids were in high school and would leave us soon anyway. I was there for them when they needed me most. I would still be in their lives, just in a different way living on my own. It was also important for me to stay friends with Sam. I did not dislike or hate him at all, we were just dysfunctional together. In other words, we were not good "marriage material" because of the different values we hold and Sam being a high "D" off the Richter scale, which comes with its own complications, like being inflexible and overbearing most of the time. Yet, Sam and the kids were my family. I did not want to lose any one of them, even though our family life had been very challenging, we never left the tiger cage, if you know what I mean.

To move on, I needed to feed the lion some food that would make him stronger so that he could get up on his feet and fight again. The old buddy of mine that I had nearly forgotten about resurfaced to remind me that "I can and I will push through this challenging time" if I put my mind to it. And so I did, I started to focus on the affirmation that has helped me many times before. Just like in school I repeated "I can and I will" over and over again to engrave it in my mind. It worked and empowered me to take my life back in my hands.

Even though I left, I still kept believing one day things could be different for us, and I am grateful I was right. Our kids have turned into wonderful and amazing young adults. I am very proud of them, and I am proud to be their mom. I am also grateful Sam and I are still friends, because that provides a more solid foundation for our children to spring from. As strange as it may sound, our "tiger cage" has turned into a "cuddling bear" reserve. We all get along great and enjoy spending time together, for which I am filled with gratitude.

While it was not the "wrong choice" when I married Sam and became part of the family, it was not the "right choice" for the long run. More so, I learned about the importance of defining and paying attention to your values. Whether you realize it or not, values exist, and as mentioned above, they contribute to the overall satisfaction of your life. When you live by your values, you feel good about yourself, and you are likely to stay more focused on doing what's important to you. When you compromise your values for any reason, things will feel wrong and can cause stress and unhappiness in your life. With that, let me share tool #5 with you.

TOOL #5: Define Your Core Values

Defining your core values will help you to uncover who you truly are so you can live in alignment with your true self and what you believe is right or wrong. When you stay aligned with your values—which means your intentions, words, thoughts, and actions support your values—you are able to live a life that's meaningful and filled with passion, purpose, creativity, happiness, and peace of mind. When you compromise your values to fit in or keep the peace, like I did, or for any other reason, you are actually betraying yourself. Not being true to yourself means compromising your happiness. It will only make you feel bad, sad, ashamed, alone, disappointed in yourself, or emotionally drained and traumatized.

Staying true to yourself is one of the keys to happiness and living a life you love. That's why it's important to define your values. Once you know what your values are, you can make decisions that honor them, avoid costly mistakes, reduce stress, and stay true to yourself. Knowing your values will help you to recognize when you are compromising your integrity.

Before we talk about how to define your values, let's review what core values are. As we discussed, your core values are the fundamental beliefs, standards, or moral principles you live by. They are the things that are most important to you. By "thing" I am not talking about your car or house, I am talking about the guiding principles you live by, the characteristics and behaviors that "sit well with you."

Think in terms of:
- What brings you joy?
- What gives meaning to your life?
- What can't you live without?

You can also determine some of the values that are important to you by thinking of things that bother you and make you uncomfortable or angry. These feelings can be triggered by your own behavior or someone else's. For example, if you've told a sweet little lie to get by a certain situation, you might not feel so good afterward because you value "Honesty." Or you might have a colleague that says and does whatever it takes to make a deal, without much consideration for others. This behavior bothers you because you may value "Cooperation" or "Empathy" or "Friendliness."

You see, each value relates to certain behaviors, like "Honesty" relates to telling the truth and acting truthfully. When the behavior is aligned with the value, it feels right to us. When it does not align with the value, it feels wrong. So, we can determine values both ways, by what feels right and by what feels wrong. Does that make sense? Let's take a closer look at both scenarios.

PUTTING THIS TOOL INTO ACTION

What Feels Right?

When thinking of the core values that are important to you, think about what brings joy and meaning to your life. What "sits well with you?" What makes you happy and fulfilled? What gives you purpose? And what supports your vision for yourself? Think about your life, your choices, your actions—what are some of the deep, underlying motivations that drive you?

Think about situations in which you feel real and your most authentic self (consider situations from both your personal as well as your work life). Answering this question will give you a clue as to what times you are most in alignment with your values. Now, think of what's going on in those situations. Here are some statements for you to complete:

It feels right, when I am with (people who you feel drawn to, are energized by, or who inspire you) _____

_____

_____

_____

_____

It feels right, when I am doing (activities that bring you joy)

_____

_____

_____

_____

_____

I feel (proud, happy, fulfilled etc.) _____ when I am (a way of being, like supportive, loving, caring etc.) _____

_____

_____

_____

_____

_____

Ask yourself in which way these situations and experiences give your life meaning and/or contribute to your passion, purpose, happiness, and peace of mind?

What value(s) might be associated with the situations that feel right to you?

The simplest way to get you started is to look at a list of values. Here is a short list, but you could also check out a more complete list of values on the internet at https://www.cmu.edu/career/documents/my-career-path-activities/values-exercise.pdf. Since things on the internet change daily, the link may no longer work when reading this book. Simply search for a list of core values, and you'll see tons of them show up in your search results.

Honesty - telling the truth

Peace - avoiding conflict

Compassion - understanding other people's needs

Integrity - staying true to your word and walking your talk

Power - being in control, dictating, and/or dominating others

Kindness - being nice, putting other people's needs before yours

Empathy - having concern for other people's feelings

Independence - doing things your way, standing on your own

Family - caring about parents, siblings, children, and relatives

Loyalty – valuing relationship and reciprocity

Commitment – finishing what you started

Adventure – doing things that are exciting and can be dangerous

Generosity – giving without the expectation of return or reward

Write the values that are important to you down here:

_____

_____

_____

_____

_____

_____

_____

Once you have defined the values that are associated with situations that feel right to you, let's complete the same statements for situations in which you don't feel like your most authentic self. This will help you to clarify at what times you might be compromising these values.

What Feels Wrong?

It feels wrong, when I am with (people who irritate you, upset you, put you down, make you angry, or just simply don't "sit well with you") _____

_____

_____

_____

_____

It feels wrong, when I am doing (activities you do to keep the peace or because you are told to, and the like) _____

_____

_____

_____

_____

I feel (uncomfortable, sad, angry, mad, ashamed etc.)_____ when I am (a way of being, like giving in, keeping quiet, not standing up for myself, being weak, etc.)_____

_____

_____

_____

_____

Defining your values both ways, like what feels right and what feels wrong, will help you understand at what times you live according to your values and at what times you compromise them.

Once you have the values established that are important to you, it's helpful to prioritize them to see which values mean the most to you. This will help you to live by them with Integrity and use them to make decisions.

For each value on your list, rate whether that value is:
- Extremely important to you
- Important to you
- Somewhat important to you

"Integrity" is the highest value on my priority list It comes before all other values. It's extremely important to me to live with Integrity, which for me means "say what you mean and walk your talk." That is why it's always bothered me when people stay together pretending their world is at peace and everything is fine, but as soon as you leave their house, it turns into a war zone. Or when people tell me, or anyone else, they are going to do something, but they don't mean it and consequently don't do it. I tend to distance myself from people with these traits as I find their behavior disturbing. It bothers me and does not sit well with me. However, it's harder when it happens in your personal relationships or at work.

While I am not an advocate for getting divorced, I also don't believe it's healthy for a couple to stay together because of an "until death do us part" commitment. I lost friends over my first divorce in Germany because they did not understand how I could leave a relationship I had made a commitment to.

"Commitment" is on my value list under the important category, but "Integrity" is up one category under extremely important. If I have to break a commitment, I feel bad about it, but if I compromise my integrity, I am not staying true to myself, and that hurts me more than breaking a commitment. Sometimes after making a commitment, you go through a period I call "Discovery." During this "Discovery," you may find everything is not as you thought it was when you first made your commitment. This is not an excuse not to stay true to your word, but there are times when you need to put your well-being ahead of other things in life, even some of the values you carry. Can you see how establishing and prioritizing your values can influence your decision making?

Establishing and defining your values can be a challenging exercise. Don't worry about coming up with the "perfect" list at this moment, just enjoy the process and see what you get from it. The idea behind this exercise is to enable you to live according to your values, make decisions with confidence and clarity, and get rid of what pulls you down, so you can feel great and live happily and fulfilled.

Values can change over time, and that's okay. While monetary things may have been very important to you at one point in your life, they may not be as important to you today. Or perhaps while being the best and/or successful professionally was important to you in the past, now your family life and time off has become more important. You will discover more thoughts and emotions as you grow older, gain life experience, and spend more time thinking about what's important to you. It is for that reason you should revisit your values throughout your life, particularly when you encounter a stressful situation over a long period of time and can't quite figure out why. Perhaps you are not living in alignment with your values and started compromising them for whatever reason.

So, let's see: What values are in your treasure box?

Here is your ACTION STEP for this tool.
Use it now!

Pick one to three of your core values you would like to make a priority in your life right now. Next, identify what behaviors would support these values. For example, if you choose Health and Wellness, ask yourself which day-to-day actions would help you stay aligned with that value (i.e., eating nutritious food, exercising, getting sufficient sleep, avoiding "bad" habits, such as smoking and drinking too much).

Write each value and the associated behaviors and actions on index cards and keep them handy to review often. You can keep them at your bedside, stick them on your bathroom mirror or your vision board, place them on your desk or wherever you can easily see them each day. When looking at your index cards and the values that are important to you, ask yourself:

What can I do to better align myself with these values so I see/feel a notable change?

It's not hard to make decisions once you know what your values are.
~Roy E. Disney

CHAPTER 6

Conquer anxiety and experience inner peace

S am and I got divorced in record time. I don't even know how this was possible, since you normally have to live apart for a certain period of time. But in typical Sam fashion, he pulled some strings and made it happen. Chapter closed! However, we decided to keep working together because we had built a real estate business that was generating sufficient leads to keep us both busy. Besides that, he appreciated my help, and I was thankful for the financial security since Sam was paying me a set amount for my work each month, and I was earning commissions whenever I sold a house. While working together was challenging at first after the emotional rollercoaster we both went through in our divorce, it worked for us for the next eight years.

I had enough money for a down payment on a home and was able to purchase a nice little house in town close to my work. Sam helped me with the transaction since it was his listing, which I much appreciated. This created a secure environment for me to move on with my personal life. After settling into my new home, I went out on a date with Jack, the man I am married to today. Jack and I had known each other through work for over eight years. It just happened that we both got divorced within a year of each other and found ourselves in the dating pool at the same time. With Jack already knowing me professionally, he felt I would be a safe bet for his first date. Little did he know I would be his only date. We are so aligned in our values that once we got to know each other outside of business, we never wanted to leave each other's side. Our compatibility extends beyond our values and includes things like what we consider fun, the foods we like to eat, the friends we like to keep, and the adventurous lifestyle we both like to live.

After dating for over a year, we decided to move in together. We spent the first few months in my house and then, to my surprise, had an opportunity to move into Jack's log house on five acres out in the country. Jack's ex-wife was living there with two of their three children after the divorce. The deal was that they split the payment while she was living there. When she got tired of the large monthly expense that was associated with living in the log home, she decided to move in with her girlfriend who had a big house to the South. Not that Jack or I could afford the payment and utilities at the time either. We were in the middle of a real estate crash, and he was a mortgage loan officer who relied on home sales for a living. So did I as a realtor. But in lieu of the house going into foreclosure because it was "underwater," Jack decided to move in using his retirement savings to enable him to make the house payments as well as the child and spousal support.

This was very difficult emotionally and financially as he owed a couple hundred thousand dollars more on the house than it was worth. Jack chose to do this because of his values. He made a commitment when he purchased the house to repay the money he had borrowed. He felt that as long as he had money, like his retirement account, he would continue to make the payments to follow through on his obligation.

Many of his friends and peers suggested he was stupid for doing this and should have used the divorce as an opportunity to clean the slate of this negative equity that was created by the housing crash. While keeping the house was a costly financial move, Jack felt he would be morally bankrupt if he took this easy way out. Commitment is a core value Jack and I both hold, so I supported him in his decision. We moved into the log home and turned my home into a rental.

The first five years were very difficult for us. This "cabin" was a 4,300 square foot log house with 18-foot vaulted ceilings in the living room and 14-foot ceilings in the master suite. While spectacular, imagine heating this house during the Pacific Northwest winters. We kept the thermostat under sixty degrees and opted to put on extra clothes to keep warm. The wood stove in the dining room managed to keep the kitchen a little warmer, but the living room was simply off-limits without a parka. The greatest thing for us at the time was the mattress heater we purchased. It was way cheaper than heating up the master suite and enabled us to jump into bed without freezing. Every time we would climb into bed, we rejoiced and triumphed over our warm bed. It made us smile despite the freezing temperatures in the room.

This was a time of financial hardship that we would not wish on anyone. We both watched our financial resources, income, and savings shrink, while our credit card debt went up substantially to enable us to maintain the house and pay all our other bills. Even though it was hard, we worked through this time because we truly believed things would get better. And they did, but it took a long, long time!

What carried us through was our positive vision of the future and our sincere belief we could make this happen. So, what is "this" you might ask? It was our vision of an idyllic life in the country with beautiful flower gardens, fruit orchards, berry patches, and loving animals surrounding us. We accepted our current situation but continued to focus on our mutual dreams and goals. Jack and I believe worrying about a situation that is challenging is wasted energy. Instead, we put our energy into the day-to-day tasks that are required to move on. We both have the same mindset: "It is what it is, let's make the best out of it."

We don't let adversity rain on our parade, instead we put our focus on the positives and remedies. We simply handle things as they come our way. We always have goals and plan for the future. We believe we can achieve our goals if we focus on them, one day, one moment at a time. We don't dwell on the past as it can't be altered anyway, and we don't worry about the future as the future is unclear and not promised to any one of us. However, we both dream about and plan for the future. Remember, what you focus on expands. All I can say is I have experienced the truths of this statement several times in my life and continue to experience it more and more. It makes me want to dream bigger to allow greater things to come through, just like Jack's audacious dream that came through for us about two years ago, which I will talk about in Chapter 9.

While we both live a very harmonious life together and deal with challenges as they come, we function slightly different, which sometimes creates a bit of conflict. It has to do with our personality types and the way we "operate" in general. We are both "I" types, which as you may remember stands for "Influence" and describes people that are sociable, talkative, and lively. In that aspect we fit very well together. We also have some "D" characteristics, which helps us in our business ventures, so another good fit. However, I am more focused on work and tend to plow through the fields like an ox with an attitude of "don't mess with me, I got shit to do." I realize this is not the best way, as I stress myself out unnecessarily as well as those around me. I concentrate so much on the work in front of me and all the things that need to be done that taking a break never even crosses my mind.

For me, there is always more to do than there are hours in the day, so I keep on working to get the stuff done on my never-ending to-do list. This is very exhausting, to say the least.

Jack, on the other hand, leads a more balanced life taking time to smell the roses. His life is way more at ease and at peace. He simply does not worry about how much work there is to do, it will get done in a "timely fashion." Even under great pressure, Jack manages to look like he is on vacation. He constantly fantasizes about the future while I focus on the present. He gets things done, but in a more leisurely way, which used to upset me especially when we were in a time crunch. I considered this "frivolous behavior," dreaming about something when we needed to focus on the task at hand. What really can get me going is that Jack sometimes stops working altogether and starts thinking out loud about his visions for the future. *Seriously, stop fantasizing dude, and let's get to work* is what I think in those moments. Worse is when he insists on taking a "time out" to do whatever nurtures his mind and body for however long he needs it. Oh my gosh, I can lose my marbles over that! How can you sit and read or watch a fishing video when work is piling up around you?

Here is what I've come to learn. While most people admire me and my work ethic, Jack's way of dealing with challenges and day-to-day requirements is by far healthier than mine. I can easily work myself up, get annoyed, and let the stress get to me. Jack has empathy and complete acceptance of whatever difficult situation he faces, which enables him to live a much more peaceful and idyllic life. He takes the time to live in the moment because he charges his batteries this way. While my batteries run out of juice every so often, Jack's are always charged up. His life is way more balanced than mine because of his demeanor. Nobody and nothing seem to rattle his chain. While I am not afraid of dealing with challenges, they tend to rattle my chain and get me worked up. I will plow through them, but I would like to learn how to handle these situations more gracefully, not like an ox. I want to be less of a workhorse and more of a collaborator like Jack. I want to live more in the moment, like him, and take time to smell the roses to eliminate the stress I put on myself.

How about you? Are you taking time to recharge your batteries or are you like me, working endlessly until you drop exhausted into bed? Would you like to experience less stress and more peace, but don't know how to achieve it?

Feeling at peace, happy, and content is something we would all like to experience yet it seems so hard to attain in the fast-paced world we live in. No matter how hard we try to lower our level of stress and anxiety, there always seems to be something new crossing our path that throws us a curve. It's easy to get lost in all that bombards us on a day- to-day basis. The constant battle of dealing with curveballs can be exhausting. We hear that one should learn how to create balance and live in the moment because people who do appear to be happier and healthier. Health and happiness are what we all desire in our lives, but how is "Work Life Balance" possible? How can we live in the moment? Let's take a look at tool #6.

TOOL #6: Strive for Balance and Live in the Moment

As you can see, this tool has two key elements: learning how to balance your life and live in the moment. For me, the two belong together when it comes to conquering anxiety and experiencing inner peace. It's hard to live in the moment without reallocating your time and energy to the things that are most important to you and lift you up. However, each component has a slightly different meaning and steps to achieve them. I'd like to peel the two apart, and look at both separately. What does each part mean and how can we achieve it?

Let's start by taking a closer look at the meaning of "living in the moment"

For me, living in the moment means all of your attention is focused on the present, the here and now. It means you are aware and mindful of what is happening around you, all your senses are engaged. Nothing else matters, you indulge fully in the moment at hand and enjoy the experiences each moment has to offer. Often, we are physically present, but our mind is somewhere else. When we are mindful of what is happening in the present, we expand our awareness and see things more objectively rather than letting our emotions get a hold of us or our preconceived ideas influence our actions. Living in the moment means savoring what's in front of us, not worrying about the future and what could go wrong. Neither is it dwelling on the past, on painful experiences, on difficult times, or perceived wrongs by us or others. Most of us tend to get sucked into the past or the future or the never-ending to-dos and are so occupied with and distracted by our work, worries, fears, regrets, and anger that we don't pay attention to the moment at hand. We may not realize it, but dwelling on the past can be depressing and create a lack of enthusiasm in us, while worrying about the future can cause a lot of stress and anxiety in our lives, not to mention the workloads we put on ourselves that can also create an abundance of stress.

That is why being present minded is so important. When we live in the moment, when we focus on the now and savor what's in front of us, worrying melts away, ruminating ceases, and our stress level decreases. We become more connected with our thoughts, feelings, and surroundings. We feel more alive and at peace. Have you ever stopped at a flower and smelled its fragrance? What about breathing in the fresh air after a rainfall? How about stopping to watch a hummingbird slurping the nectar from the feeder you put out or taking a five-minute break in the middle of your busy day to enjoy the sunshine outside? Think back to the last time you did something like this. Do you remember how it felt? I doubt you worried or experienced fear in that very moment. Most of us would enjoy such moments feeling happy and content, even if it's just for a short time. Would you agree? That's what living in the moment means to me, yet I barely allow myself to do it because of all the things that constantly seem to occupy my mind. How about you? Where do you fit in this picture? How often do you allow yourself to "seize the moment and smell the roses?"

Before we talk about "how to seize the moment at hand," let's turn to the second component of this chapter's tool, the "balancing act."

What is the meaning of "balanced living"?

Our lifestyle is composed of a variety of elements: Family/Parenting, Work/Profession, Finances, Health and Well-being, Intimate and Social Relationships, Fun and Enjoyment, and Spirituality. For me, living a balanced life means considering all the above-mentioned elements of life and allocating my time to those that are most important to me. It does not mean giving equal time to all things. It means determining what gives meaning to your life what lifts you up, what fuels you with energy, and what brings you freedom and peace of mind, and then expanding your time and energy in those areas. Likewise, you need to determine which aspects don't mean as much to you so you can reduce the time you spend in these areas. This will look differently for every one of us. There is no one size fits all model or mass-producible solution. We all have different needs and desires, thus it's important for you to find your unique life balance.

Let's face it, creating balance in our life is one of the greatest battles we will ever fight, yet it's crucial for our well-being. Life feels better when we are in good physical health and feel fit, enthusiastic, and full of energy. Life feels better when we are able to express our creativity, enjoy emotional and psychological stability, have harmonious relationships, feel financially stable, know how to effectively deal with stress, and have a sense of purpose and meaning in life. Would you agree? But how to get to that point is the question. How can we create a balanced lifestyle and live a life that feels good to us?

PUTTING THIS TOOL INTO ACTION

Let's first investigate how to create balance in our life, then we'll discuss how to seize the moment and smell the roses as often as we can.

How can we strive for balance?

1. Determine where you are off-balance

First, you need to determine in which areas of your life you might be off-balance. Where do you juggle most of your balls? In other words, spend most of your time? Let's take a pen and go through the list below giving each area a number from 1 to 10, with one being the least amount of time spent and 10 being the most. Circle the number for each area.

Family / Parenting	1 2 3 4 5 6 7 8 9 10
Work / Career / Profession	1 2 3 4 5 6 7 8 9 10
Personal Finances	1 2 3 4 5 6 7 8 9 10
Health / Wellbeing / Exercise / Nutrition	1 2 3 4 5 6 7 8 9 10
Intimate & Social Relationships / Friends	1 2 3 4 5 6 7 8 9 10
Fun / Enjoyment / Relaxation	1 2 3 4 5 6 7 8 9 10
Spirituality / God / Church	1 2 3 4 5 6 7 8 9 10
Personal Development / Education	1 2 3 4 5 6 7 8 9 10

Now, let's see how satisfied you are with your results. Is where you are in any of these areas where you actually want to be? Scale each area again from 1 to 10, this time with your level of satisfaction, one being not satisfied at all and 10 being very satisfied. Perhaps use a different colored pen to see the difference. The above exercise is a good start to see in which areas you feel unbalanced. If you like, you could highlight the areas you are unbalanced as reference so you can start working on them.

Once you have completed the exercise, you will have a better understanding of where you are lacking. With this information you can make a conscious decision to focus more on the aspects of your life that are not receiving enough attention. Creating balance in your life takes effort on your part, thus you really need to want it. Talking about being stressed out and having too much on your schedule is one thing, being committed to making a change is another. You are in charge, it's your choice to commit to the changes that are required to bring more joy and happiness into your life.

2. Set Boundaries

Now comes the tricky part. We need to set boundaries and learn how to say "NO," knowing we are saying yes to something else we want. We need to determine our priorities and clarify what's essential or adds value to our life versus all the nonessential things that solicit our time. Many of us take less time or no time at all for things that recharge our batteries, instead we let them run out of juice. Burnout is next on the list if we don't watch it. That is why learning how to remove the parts of our life that take up too much space yet don't give us the results we desire, is crucial. Setting boundaries, and saying "NO" is part of the removal process. Here is where values come back into place.

When determining your priorities, follow your values and decide what's truly important to you. Is it work, school, building a business or training for something, your family and friends, your health and well-being, your spiritual alignment, or your engagement and support in an organization? Trying to be a "jack of all trades" to anything and everything not only robs you of your precious time, but is a recipe for burnout. Saying "NO" is one of the hardest things to do with all the opportunities that get thrown at us on a daily basis. However, YOU CAN DO IT with some effort, planning, and goal setting. We will talk about planning, goal setting, and building your "No System" in more detail in Chapter 9.

3. Be Flexible
It's also important to be flexible and go with the flow. The best made plans don't always work out, stuff happens, crises enter our lives, and responsibilities need to be dealt with. That's life, isn't it? Preparing our minds for those unexpected moments and learning how to roll with the punches when things happen that we have no control over, will enable us to experience less stress in those situations. So, if you get stuck in traffic, your computer stops working, your power goes out, or you get sick when you really can't afford getting sick, acknowledge the situation, then take a deep breath and say, "O.K. What's Next? Let's see how I can jump over this hurdle.". That's keeping a positive mindset in a challenging situation. I know it's easier said than done, but trust me, there is a way we can learn to control our habitual tendencies, which brings me to the next point.

4. Live Consciously and with More Intention
How we look at the world and the things that happen around us affects the way we deal with any given situation in our daily life as

well as when we experience stress. Throughout my coaching training with iPEC, the Institute for Professional Excellence in Coaching, I've learned about "Energy Leadership," which is a style of leadership we all can adopt into our lives. Whether you think of yourself as a leader or not, you are one! You are the pilot of your own life. The question is how well do you have your plane under control? How balanced are you moving through the air? And how do you handle turbulence, wind shear, and storms?

Energy Leadership helps us become more aware of our thoughts, emotions and actions. With awareness and understanding we can live with more intention and make choices as to how we want to act in any given situation versus simply reacting out of habit. Energy Leadership is about conscious action versus reaction. It's a frame of mind that has transformed my life for the better, and it can transform your life too. I can't wait to share it with you in Chapter 8.

For now, let's see how we can live mindfully in the present and savor the moments at hand in a world that continuously draws our attention to past problems, future issues, or the things that need to be done to fix what needs fixing.

How to "live in the moment"

Living mindfully and in the present moment is a challenging task. Life seems to be an ongoing Marathon that requires a Sprint every now and then, so how can you possibly slow down and live in the moment? And how can you not worry about tomorrow? The media certainly does not help us to concentrate on the moment at hand as it constantly puts worry and fear into our minds. It's also understandable for us to dwell on the past and things that did not work out, but we can't let those thoughts or outside influences control our lives if we truly want to be happy and feel content, fulfilled, and at peace. So, let's tackle both—our worries about potential future issues and our struggles with past experiences.

Not worrying about the future

One of the bigger challenges most of us face is spending too much time on the "What If?" question. This question seems to take up a lot of precious space that could be filled with more productive thoughts. For that reason, we need to tame the "What If?" question and kick it away. It's another one of those things that's easier said than done, but we can do it! We need to stop worrying about the future as it's neither guaranteed nor in our control, but we still need to think and plan for the future and prepare ourselves for what surprising challenges the future may bring.

There is a big difference between dreaming of and planning for the future compared to worrying about it. So, let's think this through for a moment. What is it that we worry about? We tend to create a bunch of possible scenarios in our mind that often don't even come true. We basically worry about things that don't exist at the moment, but possibly could exist in the future. By doing so, we spend our precious energy on something that's unlikely to happen. The things we make up in our mind don't exist until they actually exist. Does that make sense? So, we need to save our energy for when it's needed, when a curveball actually gets thrown our way versus wasting it when it's just a possible scenario in our mind. Also, remember "what you focus on expands," whether that's positive or negative. This means when you worry about things, you are thinking about something negatively. These negative thoughts have the potential to draw into your life exactly what you don't want. All the more reason to tame the "what if" question.

To do so, we need to train our brain to think *no matter what will hit me tomorrow, I am not going to worry about it now. I will figure it out when the time comes.* Worrying today for what may or may not come tomorrow takes up a lot of emotional space. It hinders us from enjoying the moment we have at hand. Let's face it, the future often comes differently than we anticipated. Not worrying about it frees you up! So why not wait to see what tomorrow brings instead of worrying about it today and wasting all that precious energy that we could put toward enjoying the present? Yes, tomorrow might bring a challenge that you need to face, but what if it doesn't? What if tomorrow is going to be wonderful and things go right instead of wrong? Wouldn't that be exciting? Why not take that approach and think of tomorrow as a new day with new opportunities? It's like the saying "have a great day" versus "make it a great day." The first saying is about being reactive while the second is being proactive. Makes sense?

So, whenever the "what if" question surfaces, you could counter it with a statement like: "I will find my way. Tomorrow is a new day with new opportunities." Highlight the sentence if you like and memorize it, then say it out loud whenever you worry about the next step or tomorrow.

Even if you should encounter a challenge, if you see it as an opportunity for growth and to strengthen yourself and your problem-solving skills, you don't give worries any chance to manifest themselves. I truly believe we are all stronger than we think we are and can handle way more than we think we can. So, when the time comes, approach the challenge, but if there is no challenge in front of you there is no reason to worry about it.

Accepting the Past to Move On

The flip side of worrying about the future is living with regrets and dwelling on yesterday. We need to stop regretting and dwelling on the past because the past can't be altered. It happened and there is nothing we can do to change it. Instead, we need to learn to accept it for what it is, start where we are, and stretch forth to make changes for a better tomorrow. It's not about forgetting the past, but coming to terms with it, learning from it, and creating meaningful moments in the present that ultimately will outweigh the painful experiences, perceived wrongs, or difficult times from the past. This will help us to let go of what can't be changed and concentrate on the things we can change. I'll talk more about letting go of the past in the next chapter.

When we start realizing the present moment is truly all we ever have, we are opening the door to "present moment living." When we seize each moment in time, as it occurs, we allow ourselves to immerse in it and discover its beauty and wonder. We allow that moment to become more meaningful. When we live in the moment, we take care of ourselves and nurture our body and soul. It's not only the key to a happy and healthy life, but it also enables us to deal with stress and negative emotions like fear and anger more effectively because we are more at ease and peace with ourselves and the world around us.

Here are some **practical use-it-today ways** for living mindfully in the moment:

- Gratitude
  Develop an attitude of Gratitude. Stop a few times a day and take a mindful moment of gratitude. Value and appreciate the present moment like a gift you just received. This is one of my favorite tools, it gives me so much joy and warms my heart thinking of something I am grateful for. I am being more mindful these days and stop more often to give gratitude.

- Enjoy
  Instead of rushing through your work to get it done, engage in it and enjoy what you are doing, even if it's something you

don't like to do. Beauty can be found in anything if you open up your mind to it. Gosh, cleaning is not something I like doing, nor is ironing shirts. We all have things we don't like having to do. To make the tasks more enjoyable, I'll put music on and sing along, or I'll listen to a podcast. All of a sudden, the task is not that bad anymore.

- Breathe
Join a class or attend a training to learn how to relax and be present in each moment, like breathwork, meditation, or yoga. Some people use gardening as meditation or creating in an art class. I am still working on this one to integrate it more into my life. Whenever I do, I feel great and truly present in the moment.

- Observe
Start to intentionally notice your surroundings, and take a few moments each day to listen to the sounds of nature, and take in the smells, the sights, and the ambiance. I love, love, love doing this, it gives me so much joy. It's the easiest of all for me to do, stopping my work and watching a seagull snatch fallen chips, or a seal mama playing with her baby, or smelling the fresh air in the morning after a rainfall. Not on the water, how about a leaf blowing down the street or raindrops on a window?

- Relax and Unplug
Give yourself time to sit back and relax no matter how busy your day seems to be. Turn off your phone and be unreachable for a few moments. Remember, you get to live each moment once, that's it. Enjoy as many as you can, you will not get a second chance! I am working on this one, too!

- Follow Your Passion
  Remember, it's part of my secret sauce on how I approach life. Take time to pursue your hobbies and do what's exciting. Go exercise for twenty minutes, read for a while, take a walk, or ride your bike…whatever you enjoy doing. Don't compromise what's important to you because of time constraints. Every day I am making time to write this book no matter how much work is waiting for me. It exciting to me and makes me as "happy as a seagull with a French fry," which is the statement on a Life Is Good t-shirt I recently bought. My friends and children laugh when they see me wearing the shirt and say, "Oh, that's so you Kerstin."

- Ease Your Mind
  Listen to music if that eases your mind or just sit, be still, and enjoy silence. Sitting still is not my thing, but I like to listen to music while taking a walk on the beach or in the park.

- Savor
  This one is especially hard for me and I need to remind myself all the time: Savor your food and don't gobble it down like someone is after it. Taste and enjoy each bite; it's healthier, too. Well, that's a challenge for me I admit—I adapted the habit of eating too fast from my mother.

Which of these ways would work for you to counteract some of the stress in your life and live more mindfully in the moment?

Learning to live mindfully in the present takes time and requires vigilance. I speak out of experience, it's something I am still working on as you can see from my comments. Even if you just pick one of the tips and start practicing, it's a start. Add to it as you can, and enjoy the journey. I am most certain you will come to love living in the moment.

Here is your ACTION STEP for this tool.
Use it now!

Pick one of the practical use-it-today ways you'd like to try and commit to using it every day for the next week (starting today). Which one did you choose? Claim it here: _____

_____

At the end of each day, make a circle around the day if you took a mindful moment for yourself, and smile thinking you actually did something good for yourself.

Monday

Tuesday

Wednesday

Thursday

Friday

Saturday

Sunday

Every moment is precious, you don't get to live it twice! With that, I encourage you to put yourself first on your to-do list not just for the coming week, but from now on moving forward.

*Living in the present moment means letting go of the past and not
waiting for the future. It means living your life consciously,
aware that each moment you breathe is a gift.*
~Oprah Winfrey

CHAPTER 7

Free yourself
from emotional baggage

A year before Jack and I got married, I received a letter from my father. As you may recall, he abandoned my mom, my sister, and me, when I was not even a year old. He had never tried to contact me, not even once, before I received that letter. I was dumbfounded when I saw it in the mailbox. Forty some years later he recognizes that I exist? That is absolutely bizarre! I wasn't interested at all in what this man had to say, so I tossed the letter in a box in my closet. Perhaps one day when I am showing the weakness of old age, I might look for the letter and read it, but not now.

I hated this man. Perhaps you remember that my parents had a bakery until my father decided to run off with the assistant that was hired to support my mother. My grandma on my father's side recommended the woman as a bakery assistant so my mother could spend more time with us kids. Grandma could never forgive herself for bringing this woman into the picture and took this grief to the grave. My grandfather worked as a pastor and wanted to quit his job because he felt he could no longer serve as the leader at the church given that his son walked out on his wife and two young children. My aunty, who I love dearly, broke all contact with her brother. It broke her heart when she was walking us through the streets as young children and our father saw us but turned around and walked the other way to avoid any contact with us. His entire family pulled together and took care of us, while my father lived a new life in the same town with the woman who was supposed to help us sell baked goods. Apparently, she demanded he break all contact with us. In her mind, he had a new family, which was true because he did not waste any time bringing more children into the world with her. He did such a good job avoiding us, I didn't even know what he looked like. Can you imagine the work and collaboration that had to occur for this to happen in a town of 80,000 people?

Growing up without a father definitely had its challenges. While my sister was made out of thin porcelain, God gave me the skin of an elephant, thus I was better equipped walking through rough terrain. I would get bruised once in a while, but compared to my sister, I managed well. Perhaps it helped that I was so young when he left, I hadn't had a chance to build a relationship with him. My sister was very fragile and broke into pieces when my father left. She was not even three years old, but it affected her tremendously all the way into adulthood. No wonder, considering she was his first child. When she was born and throughout the first few years of her life, our father carried her around, played with her in his bakery, let her climb into sugar sacks, hung her on the doorknob from his belt around her waist while she was smiling like a pancake with a face painted on it. He was a proud and loving father; unfortunately, just for a very short time.

Mother was and still is a strong woman. She managed too, even though it was not easy for her to raise two little girls while working full-time and living in communist East Germany. Top that off with her being a Christian and not swimming with the stream or obeying the dictatorship that frowned on religion. This added to our daily struggle making life all the more difficult. Mother managed it all with the help of our family and her faith. My sister was never able to handle it. It affected her entire life and that of her children later on.

I hated my father for all the suffering he caused my family, especially my sister. I know hate is a strong word, and I am not taking it lightly, but that's how I felt just thinking about him. I thought if I ever met him, I would blow up a storm and give him a big piece of my mind. Oh, was I ready for that. At any given moment in time was I prepared to give him the speech of a lifetime. Everyone in my family knew that I carried hate and resentment toward the man who fathered me. Word spread and he knew, too. I know for a fact he was afraid of ever meeting me. He met my sister in her twenties, which was like winning the lottery for her. I don't know why she always adored him all her life. I really don't get it; he dropped us like hot potatoes. It weakened her tremendously, she had no self-esteem growing up, and then dealt with other issues that later affected the children she had.

Yet, she placed our father on a silver plate and always thought he was the prize of the century. What irritated me the most was that he would continue to abandon her, even as an adult. He would invite her and her first child to his home, and after she traveled five plus hours by train with a toddler and luggage, he would not open the door. What kind of an asshole is that, huh? When she came back completely devastated, I could have killed him for this cruel behavior. This did not just happen once. My sister's need for a father figure led her to continue with this self-torture. I asked her why she could not learn from this and instead go on thinking he was the best thing since sliced bread? What can I say? I have no idea, but she always had excuses for him and still loves and adores him to this day.

As for me, things changed a few years ago at the age of 46, when I received the letter from my father. A few months after receiving that letter, I got another one. I am thinking, *what the heck?* and tossed the letter in the same direction as the first one. Then an email popped up in my mailbox, which ended up in the trash folder as quickly as I could push the delete button. It started to irritate me that all of a sudden, my father, who ignored me for all my life, appeared in the form of letters and emails. There it was, his name in my face, a name that caused my stomach to feel ill thinking of all the suffering my family endured because he abandoned us.

Weeks after receiving the email, I was talking to my mom on the phone. She said my father had called to ask her to put in a good word for him the next time we talked since I did not respond to his messages. My gosh, the guy had balls, don't you think? I couldn't believe what I heard from her. But after the letters and the emails, it sounded quite possible he had the nerve to do such a thing, which left me speechless for a minute. Not only did he intrude in my life all of a sudden, but he also had the guts to contact my mother whom he left 40 some years ago. It made me furious. She, on the other hand, with her kind and loving heart as well as her faith, looked at it differently. She would state that maybe this was all happening because his wife had passed a few years ago, and the new woman in his life supported his having contact with us. She thought I should consider talking to him and listen to what he had to say. "Sorry mom, but that's not something on my bucket list, and I don't think it ever will be, so let's change the subject. I neither want to talk about him nor consider talking to him. I still resent the guy."

It was not the last time the subject of my father would come up.

The next time I was confronted with this topic was at church. The thematic focus of the sermon was the relationship between fathers and daughters. Interestingly, it was a sermon my mother and I attended together while she was visiting Jack and me for a few weeks. Even more interesting was the fact that Pastor G. held the sermon with his teenage daughter. They were both sitting on stage talking about all the good things as well as the challenges a relationship between father and daughter entails. He was talking from his point of view, as a father, and her, as a daughter.

The word forgiveness surfaced a few times, and every time it did it was like someone hit me over the head with a baseball bat. Forgiving my father? There is no way on earth I would do that, not after all the suffering he caused the people I love. I have been to many sermons where the topic spoke to me and encouraged me to make adjustments in my life for the benefit of me and the people around me, but this was too much to ask of me. "Dear God, please don't ask me to do that. . . .this stinks, it's not fair. Why me? Why now? Why at all? My father made his own bed and as far as I'm concerned, he can die in it. Please just leave me out of the picture."

Well, He didn't. God did not leave me out of it. He placed me right back in it using Pastor G. and his daughter to ever so uniquely ask me to take that big step of forgiveness toward my father. When mom and I left the sermon, I got that look from her together with the inescapable question as to what this meant to me and what I would make out of it. I admitted the sermon was one-of-a-kind, thoughtfully crafted to irritate the shit out of me. On that note, I kindly asked her to change the subject, again.

Here is the dilemma I encountered. There is a specific worship song that happens to be one of my favorites. Part of the chorus says, "Lord, I give you my heart, I give you my soul, I live for you alone and every breath that I take, every moment I'm awake Lord, have your ways in me." The dilemma I faced was I could not sing that song without feeling out of alignment. Integrity stands very high on my value list as you know, so is "doing your best under any circumstances." There was no integrity in singing "have your ways in me," it was simply not true anymore because I was not going to forgive my father. I did not do my best either because I was not even willing to try, no way on earth. I have to admit, being asked to forgive my father has been by far one of the greatest challenges in my life, but I could not move on without working my way through it. I had to make a choice, based on my belief system and my values, not the past that made me so resentful toward my father.

Here is what helped me to tackle the battle.

I've come to learn over the past several years that what others say or do is not because of you, it's based on the projection of their own reality and their feelings, beliefs, and opinions. This means that what they say or do is based on how they see the world and what they feel and believe is right. It also depends on their personality type as to how they say things and how they act. Remember, a "High D" would say things in a much more direct (and sometimes forceful) way than an "I, S or C" personality type. At the end, it has nothing to do with you, it's the way they operate. Looking at other people's behavior this way can help us to not take their opinions or careless actions personally and by doing so, we can avoid needless suffering. I know this is hard, but truly this has helped me to distance myself from others' negligent and hurtful behavior.

Often, I get asked how I could work together with Sam for more than 8 years after being divorced and still be friends with him today. Well, it has to do with understanding the above. Regarding my father, I had taken it very personally that he abandoned my family and me. Not sure what your thoughts are here, but how can you not take something like this personally? However, looking at the situation with "a new pair of glasses," I began to see that maybe he, at the time, thought and believed this was what he wanted and needed to do, and he felt okay leaving us and moving on. He valued other things more than responsibility, commitment, and being with us, thus he left. Most of us would perceive this as cruel. He did not. It's all about perception and how we look at things. What one person perceives as "okay" can be "awful" for another.

There is a huge amount of freedom that you can experience by not taking things personally. I know it's challenging, but the power behind it can set you free as the careless comments or actions of others lose their effect and don't hurt you as much. For me, looking at my father's behavior in the way described above has helped me in the process of forgiving him. I started to realize it was not his intention to hurt us, it just happened because of his decision to leave us. It caused an injury I carried with me for nearly 50 years and was not going to heal from until I forgave him, truly and wholeheartedly.

The way to forgiveness was a long and painful journey. It was hard, it was burdensome, and it tested me to my limits, but I did my best. What I first saw as a challenge was actually an opportunity for me to decide who I truly wanted to be. Being resentful, angry, and bitter does not fit into my list of values. It never occurred to me that having those feelings toward my father would ultimately prevent me from becoming the person I wanted to be—kind, loving, compassionate, understanding, open-minded, helpful, nonjudgmental, and the list goes on.

Yes, I am all those things to a lot of people, but a lot just doesn't cut it for me. It took that sermon for me to understand. You are either in it, mean what you say, stand for and live by your values, or you are not. Half-assing it will not give you an opportunity to ultimately be happy and fulfilled. There will always be baggage that's pulling you down, even though you may have buried it deep in the ground (or in the closet) just like I did. I truly thought I had closed the chapter of my father "many moons ago" as my native friend J would say. I thought I had moved on and was going to leave it to be the way it was. Well, I learned my lesson at the sermon. Consciously, I had closed that chapter, but subconsciously it still existed and now was the time to deal with it.

So, I made the choice and decided to deal with the challenge at hand, to give it my best as I usually do, and to honor my values. Most of all my integrity with myself. I wanted to sing the song again, honestly and truthfully. Honoring the phrase "Lord have your way in me" required me dig out the baggage of resentment toward my father and turn it into forgiveness. If I am honest, it made me "grinch" at the Lord and Pastor G., but I accepted the truth and faced the challenge.

On my next visit to Germany, I agreed to meet my father. My loving, faithful, and forgiving mother arranged a visit at her house. What a brave thing to do, don't you think? It was weird and awkward at first, just as I expected it to be. But over time, I had to admit to myself that he was not a bad guy, he just made a very huge mistake by ignoring us as kids. Leaving my mom was bad enough, ignoring us hit a magnitude of 10 on the Richter scale – in my opinion anyways. But that was then, today is now, and it looks different. I made a few choices myself I know impacted others, like leaving my family behind to venture to Canada in my late twenties. My choice hugely impacted one of my nieces who I helped raise when my sister went through troubling times. My niece to this day has not recovered from her past. and I know things would be easier for her if I were still around and helped her more. But there is very little I can do living overseas, which troubles me. I often felt I left her behind just like my father left me behind, so I could not help but look in the mirror and think, *those who live in the glass house should not throw stones.* The truth hurts, but it's true. This was a big pill to swallow, but it was my own medicine that helped me allow my father into my life.

At that visit, my father learned Jack and I were getting married the next year in August and stated that it would mean everything to him if he could come to the wedding. I don't know why I said "sure," but I did. Once it was out, I could not retract what I had just said. I thought, *out of all the people I know he is the last person on earth who deserves a ticket for this special event,* but the word "sure" came out of my mouth uncontrolled. Oh well, so be it. Perhaps it's part of the forgiveness process.

My father came to the wedding and worked his ass off helping with preparation and cleanup. He wanted to show that even though he was not there for me all my life, he now cared to be present, and he treasured the fact that I let him. His new partner K. came too to show that she cared and wanted to build a relationship with us. They both made the most amazing wedding cake, which all my friends still talk about to this date. It was a round cake as big as the table made out of eight beautifully decorated wedges, each with their own flavor. We basically had eight cakes instead of one. It was a work of art that took my father and K. a whole week to craft and required us to buy another fridge because he ran out of space.

They both stayed with us for three weeks, which gave us a chance to get to know one another and build a relationship we never had. My father did not like the fact that I called him Fredo, which is not his real name. I made it up. It worked for me. His real name just made me grimace and left a bitter taste in my mouth because it reminded me of the past. Calling him dad was not an option either. He would have loved it, but I simply could not bring that word over my lips, which you may understand considering the circumstances, but he had a hard time with it. I told him if he wanted a chance in my life, he would need to be Fredo in my world, to me and to all my friends. That was my rule, that's all I could give him whether he liked it or not. And so it was, he was Fredo. Even my mom called him that, which made me smile. Perhaps that was a way for her to also be able to engage with him after all these years.

Before they flew back to Germany, my father invited Jack and me to his 70th birthday party the following year. He stated, just like before, it would mean the world to him. I said I would think about it, and so I did. I thought about whether I should go or not for months. Having him here at our wedding was one thing—my world, my rules. Going over into his world, where I would meet all his friends, not to mention my stepsisters, was something else. I wasn't interested in getting to know them! I realized that it wasn't their fault that they happened to be my stepsisters, I am just really frugal these days when it comes to whom I spend my time with, especially when I am in Germany. My visits are short and I'd like to hang with the people I know, love and will miss when I am back home in the States.

Besides all the reasons I had not to go it was mainly my ego that told me to stay put. I had to jump over my own shadow and swallow my pride to make it happen. *Oh, I can do that*, I thought. I've braved some rougher waters before. So, I bought a ticket and put the birthday party on my calendar. And then there it was…that voice. There was a voice coming from above telling me that going to the party is not good enough. I had to go further and deeper to truly forgive and have an honest relationship with my father. What the heck is that supposed to mean, "further and 'deeper?'" Isn't going good enough? Don't you hate it when you think you are doing pretty well dealing with a challenge that popped up in your life, but then "someone" or a "higher voice" tells you pretty good is not your best, and you can do better? As much as I had already made a baby step toward my father by letting him into my life, I decided to stumble forward and deal with the "further and deeper"…whatever it meant.

In my search to discover the meaning of it all, it occurred to me that all the decisions I made thus far, agreeing to meet my father in Germany and later having him come to our wedding, were made from the head, not so much from my heart. I was still half-assing the job of forgiveness. I let my father into my life, but I never told him how I felt. I just told him to be Fredo and that was it, he was a new acquaintance. Going "further and deeper" actually meant to see and accept him as my father and ultimately to truly forgive him. That was the only way we could move from a fake relationship into an honest one. That was giving my best, having integrity, and letting the Lord have his way in me. That's what it all boiled down to at the end.

I decided to write down all my thoughts and feelings that I carried with me all the years prior to meeting my father, and I decided there was no better place and time than his birthday party to speak it out loud and let it go. It took me several months to put it all in writing, months of self-discovery, and months of letting my ego subside. I read it out loud, in front of all the guests, what I had thoughtfully put on paper. It was the only way I could tell him and the world, truly and wholeheartedly, that I was ready to move on and let the past be.

Dear Fredo,

I find it almost impossible to know where to start. I was wondering for a long time whether I should say anything at all or just be a quiet guest at your party. After all, you are still a stranger to me. I don't know you very well, and I don't know what makes you tick.

Since I came a long way to be part of your special 70th birthday celebration and since it's not my style to be quiet when I have something to say, I put together a little speech to let you know what I think, how I feel, and why I am here:

*Just a few years ago I didn't want to have anything to do with
you. My speech would have been different as I had nothing but nasty
things to say to you and about you, like you were an awful father
and should be ashamed about how you walked out on us without
ever looking back. Don't worry, this is not the case. Perhaps some
of the things you will hear are rather unpleasant, but wait until the
end. It's worth it, I promise.*

What I am here to say is...

I forgive you.

*You see, despite everything that happened, I do know what it's
like to feel cared for — thanks to my mother, grandparents, aunties,
uncles, the whole family, and so many friends who were there to
support us.*

*I forgive you for not being there, because it made me stronger.
When I was younger and was asked "Where's your dad?" I always
said, "I don't have one, but I have the next best thing — grandpa."
He'd already been a dad before (your dad actually), so he knew
what I needed to be taught to be stronger and a better person.
He would put me on his lap and tell me stories. He taught me
to be strong and not to back down to anyone or anything. He
showed me I was never going to be treated anything less than a
human being and even though my father by birth walked out on
me, I still had a Heavenly Father who would always be on my
side and love me unconditionally.*

*I forgive you for not being there because that made me find new
arms to be close to. My grandmothers — luckily I had two — who loved
me very much and cared for me the best they could. They taught me
how to be respectful and honest, not to lie to anyone because lies will
eventually come to the surface, and I would suffer the consequences,
so it's not worth it. I got a spanking once from Oma, well deserved*

I must say, other than that my grandmothers loved and spoiled me rotten, which I will never forget.

I forgive you for not being a parent because mom was able to pick up the slack the best she could raising two little girls on her own while working an 8 to 5 job. I am sure she envisioned raising us differently, and I know she wanted to spend more time with us, but she had to work full time to make ends meet. It was hard on her dropping us off at kindergarten first thing in the morning, then running to the bus to get to work, and running again from the bus after work to pick us up at the end of each day. It broke her heart seeing her two little girls sitting on the bench outside waiting for her because the kindergarten would close before she could pick us up. Mom gave her all, every single day, for which I am eternally grateful. She was resourceful, kind, and hard-working. She never discussed you, our father, with us other than when we'd ask her a question and if she said something, she would speak neutral about you, not angry or mad. Through our childhood, money was scarce, but mom imbued us with self-belief, aspirations, and strength. She supported us in every way, encouraged us and loved us unconditionally. When we went on vacation, she worked her butt off to get us there and back and made sure we had the greatest time ever. She went to every event we were a part of and has pictures from every one of them. She was always there for everything and was proud of us for every memory we created. It's thanks to her and her close-knit family I became the self-reliant and strong person I am today.

Granted, the road to adulthood was long and often rocky, and the absence of a father figure affects a lot of the decisions you make. I made a lot of wrong decisions and essentially paid the price for it, learned things the hard way as people say. But I got through the tough times and came out of it wiser and stronger. I have come to terms with who I am and who I want to be.

I forgive you for not being there because I know I am a better person for it. I went to my first day of elementary school without you, I graduated high school without you, and I made it through college without you. I immigrated to a new country without knowing the language – all without your advice or support. Not having you has not defined me and my success, it pushed me and motivated me to succeed even more. Who knows if I would have become the person I am today if you would have been my father and if you would have taken care of me, my sister, and mom. Overall, I am happy that everything was the way it was.

So just remember, you didn't screw me up when you left, when you stopped being with mom and ran away with someone else. My world continued on without you. I was angry for a very long time and did not want to have anything to do with you for as long as I live. Luckily, most of us get wiser with age and we see things differently, we understand more and are capable of jumping over our own shadow. This might not be true for everyone, but it's true for me. I am nearly 50 years old, my priorities have changed and my sharp edges smoothed out with the years. I still speak my mind, but in a more thoughtful way. When it comes to you, I don't feel angry anymore. I don't believe you are a bad person. Weak, foolish – perhaps. I think you made a lot of mistakes in life and I think you've paid a high price for those mistakes. You missed out on us growing up and setting out into the world. You've gotten to know my sister a long time ago and were able to share some of her good and not so good moments in life, but you've not had the chance to enjoy the person I've become and haven't shared in my triumphs, except my wedding last summer. I am grateful you came into my life a few months before, and I am grateful I was able to let you be part of this special moment.

So, I want us to be at peace with each other. I want you to know I forgive you and want you in my life and to be part of it. I want us to enjoy the time we have ahead of us, so God will. I brought you a special gift, it's not a gift that you can touch, but you can feel it: "DAD"

When I looked up from my speech, I saw tears, a lot of tears in people's faces, people I knew and people I didn't know. I glanced at my stepsisters, they had no idea what it was like to grow up without a dad. My father, crying but smiling, walked toward me and gave me the biggest hug ever, stating that this is by far the best birthday present he ever got in his life.

Since then, we have seen each other several times, either on my visits in Germany or here at our place. My dad came a few times to help us with house, acreage, and business. The arrangement was and still is that he only comes when my mom is with us because he can't speak English and "needs" her as a security blanket when we are at work or away for a while. She agreed to it out of the goodness of her heart, so my dad and I could spend time together and get to know each other. Better later in life, than never.

I think my mother deserves a medal for being courageous, loving, kind, and good hearted. I am grateful she agreed to co-mingle with us, as it helps me to have her on my side when my dad is present. Surprisingly, we all get along famously well, and our visits are always engaging, fun, and exciting. We work hard together as there is always more to do than one can handle in a day, and we have a lot of fun together. The guy is actually quite funny and entertaining and often cracks me up with the things he says. He is also a great cook, which comes in handy around dinner time. Amongst my friends, my dad made himself a name because he bakes the most amazing cakes. Everyone loves my mom, but dad got quite popular, too. So it happens that we have a lot of gatherings at our house when my parents are here. I wonder sometimes what my grandparents would say if they could see us sitting around the table laughing together.

If I didn't face the challenge of forgiving my father and let go of the past, if I would not have made the choice to work on myself and the bitterness and resentment I carried around, I would have deprived myself of all the fun times we have had together so far. More so, I can truly say that an enormous weight was lifted off my shoulders, which freed me up to become more of the person I want to be. Not that I am there yet, but I can fly higher now and enjoy the nectar of those flowers I was not able to reach before. I am grateful for that. I am grateful I made that choice. Like an anonymous writer once said: "When you forgive, you heal. When you let go, you grow."

How about you? Do you often find yourself thinking about the past, reliving situations that happened a long time ago, and wondering how different your life would be if your past would have been different? Do you think if a certain event did not happen in your life or a certain person did not do "this" to you, your life would be less complicated, and you would not struggle as much as you do? Do you sometimes feel that if you did not fail in whatever it was you tried, you would try again, but that failure taught you a lesson, and you better stay safe rather than fall on your face again? Perhaps someone betrayed or hurt you deeply and it's hard for you to let go of the anger and resentment you feel toward that person? Or is it that promotion your colleague got and that you did not that nags on you and surfaces every time you go to work?

Whatever it may be that you experienced and can't let go of, forgive, or forget because it left a deep wound, you are not alone. Many of us struggle with past experiences that hurt us one way or another. Often, we can pull ourselves back together and move on, but sometimes a certain event simply hit us too hard and carved a deep wound in our soul that's tough to let go. It's understandable to think and feel this way, but to be free and at peace with yourself and the world around you and to enjoy life to the fullest, we must learn to let go, we must refuse to entertain old pain. As Haruki Murakami once said, "Pain is inevitable. Suffering is optional" which means we can choose the route of suffering or not. It's another challenge many of us face. How can we conquer it?

TOOL #7: Release the Past, Embrace the Future

Let's start by looking at the benefits and turn on the radio station WIFM to hear "What's In it For Me?" What's the benefit of throwing away your old baggage and getting yourself a new suitcase? Allowing your past to influence the present in a negative way is like dragging a ball and chain attached to your ankle. It's hard, exhausting, depressing, and it makes us feel like prisoners. By letting go of the things, people, or events in our lives that harmed us, by letting go of anger and resentment, we not only allow ourselves to heal, we also free up energy we can put towards creating a better life full of joy, happiness, freedom, and peace. Knowing what we can gain by letting go will help us stay more committed to the task at hand!

Now let's see how we can do it, how we can let go of what's weighing us down, and how we can embrace a glowing new future.

PUTTING THIS TOOL INTO ACTION

1. **Identify what's bogging you down from the past.** Is it a failed relationship or business endeavor you simply can't get over?

Is it anger and resentment you carry because a person left you, like my dad left me? Perhaps you are angry and frustrated because your parents or friends did not give you the attention you feel you deserved or have not been there when you needed them. Maybe it's something you did in the past that does not sit well with you and you have had a hard time forgiving yourself.

2. **Understand that the past is irreversible and can't be altered.** There is absolutely nothing you can do to change it, "It is what it is." However, the past does not define you. Your present thoughts and actions determine who you are today and who you will become in the future. While we can't go back and change the beginning, we can start where we are and control our next steps, thus changing the ending.

3. **Accept the past so you can let it go and move toward a brighter future.** By accepting the past and all the emotions associated with past events (like resentment, anger, fear, frustration, and pain), we are actually letting go of resistance. If we resist things we can't change, like the past, we not only can feel helpless and hopeless, those feelings can ultimately turn into depression. We would also lack energy and enthusiasm for the things we can change and control. I find that practicing mindfulness (making a conscious effort to focus on the present moment) is helpful in learning to accept the past. We've talked about this in Chapter 6. Another tool is meditation or sitting still and chanting a positive mantra to counter the painful thoughts of the past. I've learned chanting a mantra repeatedly can be super powerful and help to re-program your subconscious mind to accept and let go.

4. **Learn from the past,** take a lesson from every experience, and let it guide you on your journey from this day forward. Learn from the choices you made in the past that did not serve you well. Learn from failed relationships and ask yourself what caused the failure or conflict, so you can be better prepared to tackle it in the future. Think of how a certain event or experience has helped you to grow stronger, even though it was painful.

5. **Forgive those that harmed you, including yourself.** I am not saying this lightly, as you know it's one of the hardest challenges I faced in my life. But it's one of the most powerful and rewarding things we can do to free ourselves from pain and suffering that's associated with past events and experiences. Forgiveness is part of letting go. It was the puzzle piece missing in my picture of the amazing life I want to live. While forgiving is an act we perform toward others, it's also a gift we give ourselves. Forgiving someone is an act of kindness to ourselves as we lighten our emotional load and get rid of the ballast that often holds us hostage. Just think about it for a moment—anger and resentfulness are the opposite of joy and happiness. Would you agree? So, we can't be angry and resentful, yet happy and joyful at the same time. By forgiving others and ourselves, we let go of anger and resentment and by doing so, we are opening the door to happiness and joy.

6. **Condition your mind to allow change to happen.** If you believe "I can never forget that" or "I can never forgive this person," or if you think "it's a wound that never heals because it's carved too deep in my soul," then you keep focusing on the past, which undermines your efforts to live a happier life. So, it's crucial to change the negative thought pattern to a positive one, like we

talked about in Chapter 3. Harness the power of your mind and change the thoughts that don't serve you well to ones that spark joy and make you feel good. Believe things can get better for you. Use positive affirmations like, "I can, and I will let go of the past, embrace the present and focus on the future." Think of what you will gain by letting go. Thich Nhat Hanh says it short and to the point: "Letting go gives us freedom and freedom is the only condition for happiness."

If the past is weighing heavily on you and pulls you down, I encourage you to cut the negative links to your past and free yourself from the emotional heaviness so that you can live your most vibrant life. Trust yourself and do it. YOU CAN! You are in control of your life. Remember, what you choose to do today will create your tomorrow. You can decide to stay in the past or step into the future. It's your choice.

Imagine a new world filled with joy, happiness and peace, it's out there waiting for you! When cutting the chain, take a deep breath and inhale a glowing new future, then exhale the past and let it go!

"You can decide to stay in the past or step into the future. It's your choice."

~Kerstin Decook

Here is your ACTION STEP for this tool.
Use it now!

If you have trouble letting go of the past, try writing a letter to yourself or to whomever you can pinpoint where your anger, hate, hurt, and/or feelings of being unworthy etc. are coming from. Writing brings awareness! By writing your thoughts and feelings down, you are able to release them, forgive them, and free yourself from the weight of those emotions. Writing enables you to express yourself more freely and without fear. You can say what you really want to say without being afraid, you can listen to your heart and pour out on paper what it is that's hurting you deep down inside. This helps you to fully understand, grow, and move forward. You're not validating what was said or done, it's acknowledging that you forgive them or yourself.

Remember, while forgiving is an act we perform toward others, it's also a gift we give ourselves. Try it and see what happens. You may feel a tremendous sense of relief and inner peace after writing a letter. You don't have to send it, you can keep it or burn it or read it out loud to someone you trust, whatever feels right to you. It's a way of cutting the chain of burden, letting go, and moving on.

If you want to fly on the sky, you need to leave the earth. If you want to move forward, you need to let go the past that drags you down.
~Amit Ray

CHAPTER 8

Discover the transformative power of "Energy Leadership"

When Sam decided to semi-retire from real estate, it was time for me to think about my next move. Word spread within our company that I was "available," which led to my being approached by another team leader to join and manage her team. I accepted the offer, signed the contract, and moved a few doors down from my old office into my new one. It was a smooth transition. I enjoyed working with the team and being able to put all my knowledge and experience from building and managing a team with Sam into place. Within one year we doubled our number of transactions. We were moving in the right direction and had gained huge momentum which really felt great.

At the end of my first year with this new team, I was offered a position to build and manage a national sales team with another company. Never in my wildest dreams would I have thought I would be given such an opportunity. I saw this as the opportunity of a lifetime to build a sales machine from scratch that would operate nationwide. It was a chance to really test myself and see what I was capable of achieving, a chance to grow personally, and a chance to add breadth to my business knowledge. Additionally, the earning potential blew me away and was an obvious attraction.

I felt honored to be offered this position. As exciting as it was, it was also scary because it felt totally out of my comfort zone. Benjamin Franklin's quote came to mind: "An opportunity is never lost, it's simply found by someone else." If I didn't grab it, someone else would.

The only thing holding me back from saying yes immediately to the new job was the thought of leaving the familiar territory I had built around me. I was comfortable where I was. My life was pretty much dialed in. I liked my work and my colleagues. I made enough money to pay the bills, pay off my debts, and save a little. I had some flexibility with my hours and time off. I had a routine, and it worked for me. Being in my late forties, I created a comfortable nest that I had no intention of leaving. The new job would lead me into unknown territory, and the "what if" question crossed my mind several times. What if I fail or the business venture does not work out?

As soon as that question surfaced, I replaced it with "what if I'm successful, the new venture works out and we all win?" I liked that thought much better and decided to focus on it. After weighing all the pluses and minuses, it became clear my comfort zone was the only thing holding me back. I felt I could push myself harder and accomplish more. After all, there were dreams on my vision board that had not come true mainly because I had reached a comfort level and settled in. Reviewing the vision board I created more than ten years ago helped me to make the decision to get off my ass and get moving again. What was I waiting for?

If I wanted all my dreams to come true and dream even more, I would need get comfortable with the uncomfortable, just like the cold shower I suggested you try in Chapter 4. Remember, comfort resembles stagnation. While I was encouraging our agents on the team to set high goals and do what it takes to achieve them, I was settling for less because it was easier. That thought shook me up and triggered my "action button." I needed to jump, or I would stay in the same place for the rest of my life. Jack helped too and encouraged me to leave the status quo behind, as he also believed I had it in me to accomplish more.

So, I jumped ship and ventured into unknown waters. Sadly, it was a short voyage. The national sales team concept was tabled when my associates found their time and energy would be better spent focusing on their own existing ventures. The new business was demanding too much of their time. I fully understood it was a business decision and respected their need to do what was in their best interests. I was thankful for the severance package I received, which gave me time to plan for my next move. Yet, there was a natural fallout that comes when life-changing plans fall through. What was I supposed to do now? The challenge of yet another setback brought with it irritation, frustration, and anger at the world in general — followed by the almost inevitable dip into the world of self-pity. Poor me. I crashed again. Worse than feeling like a wounded bird was my anger and frustration at myself for my inability to handle this pitfall in the way I expected of myself.

I knew upfront that the new job would not be easy, and I anticipated a few bumps in the road, but I did not anticipate an emotional face-plant. I had a choice to make: get up and get going again or keep licking my wounds and feeling sorry for myself. The latter was easier and came more naturally, getting up and going again seemed much harder requiring an enormous amount of effort on my part. As you know, I had experienced setbacks a few times in my life, but this time truly challenged me. Maybe it had to do with my age. When you are nearly 50 years old and hit the surface pretty hard, it requires more strength to lift yourself off the ground. One of my friends suggested I may be going through a midlife malaise, but I rejected that idea since I knew exactly where my distress was coming from.

Once again, I needed to put myself back together. So, I've pulled out the familiar affirmation that has become my life companion and carried me through many challenges before: "I can, and I will move on," even though I had no idea at the time how to move on." All I knew is that I decided to jump ship, the voyage ended abruptly and now I needed to deal with it. I needed to take full responsibility for my actions and the choice I had made. Doing so is one of the primary elements of success.

I believe things happen for a reason. We often don't know the reason right away and sometimes never get clarity, but I still believe there is a purpose for why things happen. I also find some truth in the saying, "when one door closes, another one opens." While I am saying this—needing to take responsibility, moving on, looking for a new door to open—I don't find any of it easy. I definitely had my struggles and experienced an emotional rollercoaster ride!

One of my friends was going to sign up for coaching and threw the question my way, "Why not sign up for coaching Kerstin?" Not to *be* coached, but to *become* a coach. The idea had never crossed my mind, but the more I thought about it, the more I liked it. This door was opening and I had to choose whether to walk through it. I knew how powerful coaching could be since I had years of being professionally coached under my belt, plus I had a degree in education. I also had 15 years of real estate knowledge and experience. If I were to combine my education, knowledge, and experience with coaching skills, I could help real estate agents and other entrepreneurs in a more advanced way than I had in the past. So, why not? Why not become a coach and see where it takes me? I had already left my comfort zone, so why not move on and see what life has to offer?

I signed up with iPEC, the Institute for Professional Excellence in Coaching, and became a Certified Professional Coach and Energy Leadership Index Master Practitioner. Ironically, I was my first client and coached myself through my recent faceplant with the help of one of my coaching buddies. Even with all my practices and positive efforts, I still had not closed the chapter of the closed business venture. It kept nagging at me every time I thought about it. One of iPEC's foundational principles came in handy as it suggests seeing problems and challenges as opportunities. I guess I needed that reminder.

When I joined the business venture, I saw it as a huge opportunity to expand my management and team building skills. Instead, I became a more effective leader of my own life. What happened was a continuation of the growth I experienced when I forgave my father. I've come to learn that many of the opportunities that have found me or that I have recognized are linked together in a progression with one building upon the other. While the national sales director job did not turn into the success I expected, it brought a greater opportunity. I discovered my passion for coaching, but first and foremost I uncovered my true potential, which far exceeds my managing and team building skills. The business venture almost had to fail for me to reach a whole new level of growth. It was a hard pill to swallow at first, but it has transformed me into a better version of myself, for which I am extremely grateful.

What I learned through the Energy Leadership coaching program at iPEC has improved my life in many ways. I am so grateful for my wonderful friend who encouraged me to begin this adventure in coaching. On that note, let's dive into the next tool. It has been a life-changer for me and it can be for you too.

TOOL #8: Live with Intention, not out of Habit

When you live with intention, you are purposeful in what you say and how you act. In other words, you know why you say what you say and do what you do. There is meaning and purpose behind your words and actions. You make conscious decisions and take action based on your values and what's important to you instead of merely reacting out of habit.

When you live with intention, you are able to improve any aspect of your life, reduce stress, feel a greater sense of purpose, attract success, and create a life that's meaningful and exciting. This has come true for me, and it can come true for you, too.

The information I am about to share about Energy Leadership is my interpretation of the copyrighted work of Bruce D Schneider and the Institute for Professional Excellence in Coaching. If you're interested in learning more, I highly suggest reading Schneider's transformative book, *Energy Leadership*. Energy Leadership is a framework for personal development that positively influences and changes not only yourself, but also those with whom you interact. I spoke of this before - you may not think of yourself as a leader, but whether you do or not, you are one! You are the pilot of your own life. And as a pilot, you know how well you have your plane under control, how balanced you are moving through the air and how you are handling turbulence, wind shears, and storms? How would you answer those questions?

Maybe you are happy with your answers and feel you are flying high. That's awesome, and I applaud you for it. Maybe there's a way to hone your skills. And if you know your skills need some improvement, especially under windy or stormy conditions, let me shed some light on how you can become a better pilot so you can feel great about flying instead of feeling airsick, like I have in the past.

Energy Leadership can help you improve the way you fly your plane. That is, the way you lead your life. Energy Leadership is a unique form of personal leadership that has nothing to do with "physical energy," it's all about the "energy level you bring to life." Your energy level does not refer to how much energy you have to do something, like going on a ten-mile bike ride or running a marathon. It refers to "the way you show up in life"—your thoughts, perceptions, and behaviors in any given moment and over time. The Energy Leadership framework outlines seven levels of energy—the bottom two levels are negative types of energy that are draining and tear us down. They can potentially be destructive to us and those around us if we resonate at the lower levels over a long period of time. The upper levels, three through seven, are positive, creative, productive, constructive, expanding, fueling, healing, and growth-oriented. Those are the energy levels that build us up. People who resonate at higher levels attract more positive things experiencing greater joy, peace, success and fulfillment. Energy Leadership raises your consciousness. It helps you become aware of the energy you bring to the table, in your daily life, and when experiencing stress. With awareness and understanding, you can make new choices and decide at which energy level you want to show up in daily life and when under stress, instead of simply reacting, which is a habitual tendency of the human being.

We all have developed habitual tendencies as to how we react to certain situations, circumstances, the environment around us, etc. depending on our personality type, upbringing, previous experiences, and the beliefs we carry. Those tendencies fire without us consciously noticing them. In other words, we react the way we normally do. We continue to do the same things over and over and wonder why things don't change for us.

Energy Leadership helps us break this self-perpetuating cycle and be more at choice with our thoughts, emotions and actions in each moment. How? Let's start by taking a closer look at the different levels of energies available to us.

As mentioned above, there are seven energy levels or ways in which we can show up in life, with level 1 being the lowest and level 7 the highest. The higher the energy level the more powerful it is. For the purpose of my explanation, I will use the term "Mode," to explain the manner and energy level in which you show up at any given point.

Level 1 is "Victim Mode." We can experience this level when we feel one or more aspects of our lives are not in our control. In those moments our thoughts, beliefs, emotions, and perceptions work against us, they don't serve us well, and can result in a sense of feeling helpless or stuck. Some of the thoughts we may have when experiencing victim energy can be, "I am a loser," "I have no choice," or "Why even bother?" The emotions that could be triggered by those thoughts are fear, doubt, worry, anxiety, hopelessness, or depression.

Consequently, it is much harder for us to take action to overcome victim energy as we might experience low self-esteem and a lack of confidence. This makes it difficult to approach problems or confront the issue at hand. With enough negative energy, we can hit bottom, requiring an enormous amount of effort and willpower to pull ourselves out of. We all experience this energy level at one point or another, it's normal. So, if you feel this way at times, you are not alone.

Level 2 is "Fighter Mode." This is an energy level in which we fight for what we want. Conflict is the predominant thought, anger the leading emotion, and defiance the way we show up. People in fighter mode often operate by force and control. Their thoughts of needing to be right or having to win are triggered by feelings such as pride, greed, hatred, resentment, or blame. This can create a lot of stress and frustration, not only in their own lives, but in the lives of those around them. Sometimes we need to fight for what we want; there is nothing wrong with being a fighter once in a while. It's problematic when we operate at this level on a daily basis as it's draining, exhausting, and can alienate others. Unfortunately, this level is the predominant energy in our current culture and most workplaces, a frame on life that is driven by fear, conflict, and scarcity.

Level 3 is "Rationalizer Mode." In this mode, we begin to interpret other people's actions and the situations we encounter with more peace, learning to accept them for what they are. We take responsibility for our own thoughts, feelings, and actions. We tolerate, compromise, and cooperate out of forgiveness. But there is still some judgment found at this level, like "I can forgive you, but I would not have to do it in the first place if you had not done x, y, z." So, we might still feel a bit of level 2 energy here, but predominantly this level helps us to cope, eliminate stress, deal with disappointments, and ultimately feel empowered to move on.

Level 4 is "Caregiver Mode." When we operate out of this level, we operate out of concern for others, and we care, give, support, and help. Our actions are triggered by feelings of compassion and love. Our focus is on fixing things to make them better. We lead from the heart, not from the head, and take little personally. We still think of our personal interests, but our win also comes from the winning of others.

Level 5 is "Opportunist Mode." People operating at this energy level have a highly conscious, wide-ranging view of situations and spot possibilities and solutions everywhere. They don't see problems, only opportunities. They accept things the way they are as they believe everything has a meaning and purpose. Reconciliation is the core thought; the intention is for everyone to win. People at this level feel in control of their lives, confident, calm, and at peace no matter what happens around them. They can experience a sense of joy and fulfillment within. They are solution-focused, action-oriented, and often have an entrepreneurial mindset. You might think that sounds wonderful, but don't see any way you can operate at this level. First of all, let me remind you that what you focus on expands. If you think you can't, you won't. Secondly, all levels are available to any one of us, whether you believe this at the moment or not. Energy Leadership is all about elevating our awareness and understanding that we do have these options and ways in which we can show up. We can adapt the mindset and actions associated with any one of the 7 levels. It's up to us whether we choose to or not.

Level 6 is "Visionary Mode." At this level, we are thinking of and/or planning for the future using our imaginations, our creative sides, and our wisdom. We feel alive and connected to everyone and everything and don't judge the things that come our way. We live in a state of awe and wonder and see everything as an opportunity, including those experiences others would perceive as painful or bad. At this level, we experience joy, our intuition comes alive, we are flexible, and willing to figure things out as all experiences are valuable.

Level 7 is "Creator Mode." At this level, we are tapping into our potential to love unconditionally while being totally accepting and open-minded. We don't judge, are truly fearless, we don't concern ourselves with things that don't serve us, and we have absolute passion about all experiences. We consciously create our life in each moment using all other levels at will. Through nonjudgment and absolute passion, we are able to tap into our genius talent and create brilliant ideas out of "nothing." Some of the most powerful people in the world tap into this level. With practice, we can learn to access the higher levels that may seem out of reach at the moment.

What does this all mean to you and how can you use this information in your life to your advantage?

Each of us has a different "energetic makeup," which is a combination of the seven levels that can be different in our daily life situations versus times when we are experiencing stress. iPEC offers an Assessment, called the "Energy Leadership Index Assessment," that you can take to find out what your "energetic makeup" looks like. You will see what energy levels show up in your daily life in contrast to when you are under stress. While certain levels might be predominant for you in your daily life, your stress reaction profile can look completely different. When I did my assessment, I had an idea as to what levels would show up for me, but I was completely taken by surprise to see how high my bars were in the lower levels when I am under stress. I think of myself as being able to conquer most anything, but the question is how well am I doing it? And how long does it take me to overcome adversity?

This is where the power of Energy Leadership comes into place, my friend. It can help you be more at choice with your thoughts, emotions, and actions. The process for being more "at choice" starts with awareness of where you are and finding strategies to move out of the lower levels into the higher levels in any given moment. Those strategies will look different for different people, but the tools in this book are a good start to help you build awareness, get clear on what you want and where you want to go, and ways to help you stay on track.

PUTTING THIS TOOL INTO ACTION

Let me share with you how I used the knowledge I gained from the Energy Leadership program to help me overcome my frustration due to the recent face-plant. It's my hope that by showing how I am using Energy Leadership to my advantage; it will help you see how you can improve your overall well-being and any aspect of your life where you are dissatisfied or want to achieve your goals.

While going through the program, we were paired with other participants so we could start practicing what we were learning. I was the perfect "client" as I truly had a situation I was dealing with at the time that I was not handling very well. Perhaps it did not show on the outside, but inside I carried Level 1 and 2 energy with me. After validating the levels I resided in, we worked next on evaluating the benefits of reducing those lower level energies. It's understandable I would think and feel the way I did, but what's the advantage of remaining at those lower levels? I couldn't come up with any. This makes sense since the lower levels can tear us down if we stay in them for too long.

To reduce the lower-level energy, we thought about a response I could adopt if I were to approach the issue with Level 3 energy. What would a "Rationalizer" think? How would that person act? Here is what I came up with: There was no guarantee this new business would work out. I was not promised success. I was offered an opportunity and took it. I was not forced into it with handcuffs. I was given what I saw as a very attractive offer and chose to take it. My choice to change ships had created the challenges I was facing after the new ship sank. It was up to me to take responsibility for the choice I had made and accept the business closure for what it was. This was tough though, I admit, as my ego had gotten bruised. My ego kept me at the lower levels, while consciously I did move on and believed the closure perhaps was meant to be. Whoa, what an awakening – my ego holding me back! That discovery helped me to move on and leave Level 1 and 2 thoughts and emotions behind me.

Next, we thought it would be interesting to go up the levels and find responses for each one to see at which level I would prefer to respond. Level 3 was a much better choice than 1 and 2, but perhaps there were benefits in responding at a higher level or a combination of different levels.

At Level 4, I would think less of my personal interests and focus more on my associate's needs. To do this we thought of ways to stimulate Level 4 energy, and gratitude came to mind. At the onset, I was grateful and honored I was chosen and trusted as the most qualified person for the job. That felt pretty amazing at the time, I had just forgotten about it. Looking at the situation this way helped me to not take the decision my associates made so personally. I've talked about that previously, how to not take things personally, yet I know it's easier said than done. You have to truly understand that what others say or do is based on how they see the world and what they feel and believe is right. I needed to remind myself of it. My associates acted out of their own feelings, beliefs, and opinions, which had nothing to do with me. What they had set out to start simply did not work for them. They had to cut the strings, which I knew wasn't easy for them. Thinking about the situation from this perspective completely shifted my point of view and made me feel much better than I had previously.

Moving to Level 5, I would see possibilities and solutions instead of concentrating on problems. With reconciliation being the core thought at Level 5, I would think even though the venture ended shortly after it started, we all win at the end. I would feel in control and take focused and determined action to move forward right away. That would have been nice, if I would have had the capacity to do this at the time.

Looking at a visionary's point of view at Level 6 would mean planning for the future and using my creative side and knowledge to figure things out. I would see this business closure as an opportunity for growth and consider it valuable rather than painful. Looking back at this point, I ended up with a Level 6 resolution, it just took me a while to get there without the knowledge I have now.

If I were to tap into Level 7 energy, I would be fearless, accepting, open-minded and hopeful for the future knowing my own genius talent will guide my way forward.

Can you see how the higher I went on the energy level scale, the more empowering thoughts I had? It totally shifted my energy, which we determined is "the way we show up in life," from thinking negatively to thinking more positively and feeling empowered to move on without holding a grudge. I did not enjoy being upset and frustrated, and I wasted a lot of time. Time I would have been better served focusing my thoughts and actions on improving the future, rather than dwelling on past circumstances.

When we start living with intention, we can motivate and inspire ourselves to take positive and purposeful actions, thus becoming more effective leaders of our own lives. We can transform ourselves to be more thriving, inspired, positive, productive, and successful individuals. Becoming an "effective leader" of our own life enables us to inspire others to do the same.

Energy Leadership offers us a way of taking life-changing action by choice. No matter how old we are, when something hits us unexpectedly, we always have a choice as to how we want to (re)act. Even through the biggest dramas of life, you can choose your actions and how you are going to deal with the situation. Choosing to *act* instead of simply *reacting* puts you in control of your life and lets you create and shape it the way you want it to be! It's up to you whether you cry over spilled milk or not. You can choose to live by choice, not by habit, to make changes, not excuses, to be a victim or a winner. You can choose harmony over conflict, responsibility over blame, to care and let your ego subside. You can choose to see opportunities instead of roadblocks, choose nonjudgment over judgment, trust your intuition instead of reasoning, and you can choose to break loose and fly in the direction of your dreams. I never realized how great the freedom is in understanding we always have a choice, no matter what life throws at us.

What choices will you make, my dear reader?

Here is your ACTION STEP for this tool.
Use it now!

Play the STOP -THINK - CHOOSE game! This is how it works:

When something unexpected "hits" you or you are in a challenging situation (which can be as simple as having an argument with your spouse or a friend or craving to eat that extra piece of cake), STOP before you react like you normally would. Just STOP for a second and take a deep breath.

Then THINK it through for a moment. Think how you normally would act and if that reaction will serve you best and bring you closer to your goals. Will that reaction create a warzone, or will it create peace?

Now CHOOSE how you want to act. Do you want to act as a Victim, a Fighter, or a Rationalizer? Do you choose to be a Caregiver, Opportunistic, Visionary, or Creator? You choose!

While it may sound simple, it's actually a lifelong practice and requires constant effort, but it's worth practicing because it will change your world! If you try, but think you can't do it, take a baby step and simply start with the STOP. Practice stopping and taking a deep breath. Once you feel you have a grip on that part, add the second "THINK" portion to it, and so forth.

Here is a quick example out of my own world. A few weeks ago, a boat driver who did not pay attention to the wheel ran into our newly-renovated charter yacht, right through the door of our pilot house causing a lot of damage, while I was sitting in the salon writing this book. There it was, a test for me to "practice what I preach." So, I STOPPED for a second to catch my breath and then THOUGHT of my normal reaction to a situation like this, which was clearly the fighter mode (telling the guy what I thought about his driving and why couldn't he pay more attention to the wheel and all the trouble he is causing us now, etc.). I determined this reaction would most likely create a war of words to say the least, so I decided this is not what I wanted in my life. I want peace and harmony, no warzone, thus I CHOOSE to act as Caregiver, nurturing both the driver's as well as my "wounds." I told him how sorry I was that this happened, and I hope we can figure things out the best for both of us. I could see the surprise in his face in response to my reaction. But it was awesome to see him mirroring my reaction and how he took care of the situation in a very nice and pleasant way. I consciously created peace instead of being angry and mad, my normal habitual reaction in a situation like this. Life truly is what you make it!

Your life is a result of the choices you have made.
If you don't like your life, start making better choices.
~Zig Ziglar

CHAPTER 9

Set yourself up for success

After graduating from the coaching program and passing the test to become a "Certified Professional Coach" through iPEC, I thought about such questions as "how do I build my coaching practice?" and "how do I get paying clients who wanted to work with me?" I decided to hire a consultant who specialized in helping new coaches establish a presence in the industry by assisting with marketing and various software and online platforms. My idea was to coach in the field I knew, which was real estate. I believed I could help real estate agents elevate their business to the next level with confidence while living a balanced life. Working in the real estate industry is very competitive and often leads to agents working long hours with no personal time. While I had helped agents before when working as team manager, I felt I could now do it at a much higher level with my newfound skillsets as a coach. There was also a lot of interest coming from my network, which made me feel more comfortable focusing my marketing efforts in the real estate sector versus becoming a general business coach.

While my consultant helped me, it was still up to me to develop a plan to build my coaching practice and get clients. Creating plans, setting goals, and implementing systems is something I am very familiar with from my careers in real estate and as a social educator. So, I went to work creating both short-term and long-term goals. After putting them on paper, together with the tasks I felt were required to enable me to achieve my new goals, I created a calendar with time blocks for each activity. This was my launch platform. I was set to go, and off I went. I started working on my business plan, like a dog with a newfound bone.

Of course, this was a really large bone that took a lot of chewing. At times I was overwhelmed with the sheer magnitude of my tasks, and sometimes I felt a little bummed because things didn't work out as planned or seemed too difficult. There were moments I felt some anxiety about my new venture and even a bit of low self-esteem. "Selling" coaching is not exactly an easy task as you have nothing tangible to offer, and being new in the industry doesn't help either. As soon as those level 1 victim thoughts and feelings surfaced, I recognized them and chose to move myself out of them quickly. In those moments, I would make a conscious decision to tap into the fighter mode thinking, "I will not get what I want if I don't fight for it."

Once in Level 2 fighter mode, I would go up the ladder in my mind evaluating other ways I could approach the situation possibly as a Rationalizer, a Caregiver, an Opportunist, or a Visionary and Creator. Playing the "energy level game" helped me to quickly work my way out of feeling bummed and doubtful to feeling energized, empowered, and hopeful that I indeed could create a successful coaching business.

About five months after I started building my new business, my lovely husband threw me a "curveball" that interrupted my voyage for months to come. Jack has been a mariner for over 45 years. He got his United States Coast Guard masters license in 1984 and ever since dreamed of working in the mega yacht industry. But marriage, three children, and a shoulder injury forced him out of the trades to a desk job. While he worked in the mortgage industry for over two decades, he always had at least one boat and never stopped boating. Jack also never stopped dreaming about returning to his true passion one day. Jack's big dream was to captain a charter yacht in our local Pacific Northwest waters and Southeast Alaska. We talked about it every so often, and I could see myself "being on board." However, I did not spend the same amount of time thinking and dreaming about it, because I had dreams of my own that lingered in my mind.

Well, the day came when Jack told me it was time to turn his dream into a reality before he/we got too old. As exciting as it sounded, I was a bit troubled by it because I had just started to build my coaching business. The timing was off on my side, and I felt somewhat frustrated having put so much of my time and energy into building a new business that would now be put on the back burner. I felt level 1 energy creeping up again. I tell you, it's so easy to fall into that "victim hole." While we can't protect ourselves from it, we can recognize it and work ourselves out of it as quickly as possible, which has become a game for me. So, playing my new game, I moved up the ladder in my thoughts checking each level and the approach I would take. As soon as I was at level 5 opportunist mode (seeing adversity as an opportunity), I was ready to talk with Jack about starting a new business we both could work in while still allocating time to my coaching business. We had a long chat that day and discussed how to pull it off.

There was an enormous amount of planning involved, from finding and buying the right boat, to creating a business plan, and managing our homestead with all the plants, flowers, and animals I had accumulated over the past years. Moving forward into this new venture meant having to re-home all our animals, including my beloved horse Winston with whom I had big plans in the "dressage world," and my lover boy Wyatt, our rescue dog. There would simply be no time to care for the animals in a way I felt they deserved. Although it was emotionally trying for me, I am grateful from the bottom of my heart that I found new loving homes for all of them. It was not only a big relief, but also makes me happy every time I think about them. As hard as it was, it was time to close that chapter so a new one could open.

You may have noticed by now in reading all these stories from my life that personal change, or as some call it, reinvention, has long been a full-time job for me. After the swift transition from real estate broker and team manager to being a licensed professional coach, I was now adding to this list of careers First Mate and Chef de Cuisine on my own charter yacht. This was not exactly something on my personal development plan, but what the heck, why not become all you are capable of becoming? I just had to put a plan together that focused on the mastery of the skills I needed in my new role. I planned on integrating coaching into the charter model, it just needed to wait while I trained to be a chef and honed my boating skills. Being First Mate on a 70-footer, the boat Jack planned on buying, is quite a bit different than handling the 45-foot recreational boat that we owned at the time and planned on selling to make room for the bigger one we were purchasing to launch our new charter business.

As soon as we finished our talk about building a charter business, we started looking for the right boat that would fit our criteria and our budget. We knew what we wanted to name the boat, we just had to find it. After several months, we found our "Lady of the Sea" sitting on Lake Union in Seattle. It was love at first sight. We negotiated a favorable purchase price, went through the inspection and closing process, and then she was ours. This is when the real work started. The yacht needed a complete renovation—"refit" in nautical terms—for it to work as a small cruise ship. With budget constraints and a desire to be hands-on owners, we decided to do most of the work ourselves. Luckily Jack also used to be a boat mechanic and a boat electrician, and we are both handy when it comes to construction work (recall my story from Chapter 3 working on the roof in Tofino, Canada), so we felt comfortable and capable of pulling off the refit ourselves.

It was a massive and challenging project. We knew we had to work hard every day to turn the boat into the cruise ship we envisioned. Just as I did when starting my coaching business, we put all our short-term and long-term goals on paper with a start and a finish date. Our goal was to have the boat updated and running within one year of purchase. It was a big stretch, but we thought we could pull it off with the right tools and mindset. Next, we created to-do lists for each goal, some of them pages long. Then we prioritized the things that needed to get done. We both had several lists, so it was crucial to invest our time wisely to get to where we both wanted to be in the time-frame we set for ourselves.

For the next year, we worked hard and long hours, day in and day out, seven days a week in all weather conditions. The winter months were cold, wet, and very unpleasant. At one point there was so much snow on the docks that Jack had to dig a small walkway so we could bring in the materials we needed. Our passion and desire to work together refitting the boat and building a business together kept us going despite the struggles we encountered along the way. For example, we had a stuck valve in one of our 12-cylinder diesel engines put a hole in the piston, requiring a full "in-frame engine rebuild." We had to re-evaluate our situation and adjust our goals and timelines more than once, but we kept on moving ahead no matter how challenging it was.

While we did not finish all the projects on our lists, we got the majority of the work completed so we could achieve our initial goal to start cruising on schedule. We did not make it up to Alaska, for that was not in our plan for the first year of operation, but we hit the local waters for a summer of shakedown cruises and were able to book a few charters in the San Juan Islands to get our feet wet. After the season was over, our goal was to finish the remainder of the projects and cruise the Canadian Inside Passage to Alaska and Southeast Alaska the following year. Well, we all know about what happens to the best-laid plans. They don't always work out.

The year we were ready to cruise to Alaska happened to be 2020, the year we were all faced with the COVID-19 pandemic. Our business was greatly impacted by it. We were basically shut down completely by the restrictions put in place to limit the spread of COVID-19. This put us in a position where we had to make further adjustments to our business plan. We decided to sell our homestead and moved onto the boat full-time to help with monthly expenses, and of course we still had our ever-growing list of boat projects and maintenance. While Jack dug into the new projects, I decided to take this time of uncertainty and change as an opportunity to write the book I had wanted to write, but previously had never found the time to do it. Thus, I added to my "reinvention list," being an author.

So, here we were in uncertain times where planning does not seem to make much sense, because who knows what's going to happen in the years to come? Yet, we can't put our heads in the sand and let fear or uncertainty stop us in our tracks. Well, you could let fear stop you, the choice is up to you; or you can choose to embrace this monumental time and make it a pivot point for your life, revisit your goals, and take focused and determined action to get closer to what you want to create no matter what is happening around you. I just read a quote from Robert Herjavec, Shark on ABC's *Shark Tank* series. He said: "The people that do nothing in turbulent times are the ones who get left behind. It's better to try something, fall down, and keep going—constant forward momentum is the key." Well, I could not say it better than him. Remember, you are the leader of your own life and you have the power to lead your way through any time of uncertainty and change. I believe that those of us who step into their leadership in times of adversity will come out stronger on the other side. With that, I'd like to share with you tool #9.

TOOL #9: Develop Smart Goals and Routines

In the last chapter we talked about living with intention. If you want to achieve certain goals or have what's missing from your life right now, you need to become intentional about investing your focus, time, and energy on the activities required to get you what you want. The first step in this process is to become clear about what it is you want. Having clarity ensures your attention is focused on the areas of your life or business that matter to you most. To gain clarity, you could review your vision board from Chapter 1. If you have not had the time yet to create a vision board, I encourage you to review Chapter 1 and craft one you can refer to in the days, months, and years to come. Clarifying your vision of your ideal life and perhaps business will help you set goals that will get you from where you are now to where you want to be so you can start to put steps towards your goals into action and move in that direction.

You can also refer to Chapter 6 and the areas of your life you feel are out of balance. Perhaps you want to start there and work on an area that's important to you, yet has not received your attention as much as you've desired.

Here is a quick overview of the areas we talked about:

- Family / Parenting
- Work / Career / Profession
- Personal Finances
- Health / Wellbeing / Exercise / Nutrition
- Intimate and Social Relationships / Friends
- Fun / Enjoyment / Relaxation
- Spirituality / God / Church
- Personal Development / Education

Once you are clear about what you want more of in your life and what you want to change or accomplish, the next step is to develop an action plan. The greatest goal in the world is not going to do you any good if it's just sits on the shelf in your brain. You have to be willing to remove it from the shelf and start working on it to make it real. What's the best way to do it? I love systems and routines. They keep you organized, help you to create time to do what's important to you, build better habits, increase your productivity, stay on track, and not get thrown off by distractions or trivial things that tend to take up a lot of space throughout the day. How you invest your time directly impacts the success you'll have. Being intentional about it keeps your energy high and increases your chances of getting the results you desire.

Let's start with goal setting. When we set goals, personal or professional, it's important to be SMART about it, whether it's a short-term or a long-term goal. Don't set goals that are vague. If your target is "out of focus," it's hard to hit it. By being "SMART," we are setting goals that are Specific, Measurable, Achievable, Relevant, and Time-Oriented.

The process starts with setting a SPECIFIC goal, one that is well defined and clear. For example, a general or vague goal would be "I want to save money to buy a nicer car," and a specific goal would be "I want to have x-number of dollars in my savings account in x-months/ years so I can by the x-car I want to have" The more specific you are, the better chance you have of getting what you desire.

The next step is to make the goal MEASURABLE. This means you need to come up with a qualifier or quantifier for measuring your success. You need to set milestones along the way that will help you know the progress you are making and if you are on track to reach your goal. For example, building on the specific goal above you could come up with the following criteria: "I am going to put x-dollar each week into my savings account for the next x-months".

Next ask yourself if your goal is ACHIEVABLE and within your reach. This is a yes or no question. To help you answer the question, give yourself a serious reality check. "Do you have the skills for it? Obviously, saving money does not necessarily require a skill, but it does require a focused determination to change your spending habits. Other goals may require that you learn new skills that come from training and education. You also need to ask yourself if you have the necessary resources to achieve your goal?" If you determine the goal is not attainable at this moment in time because you may not have the skills or resources for it, think of how you could build your skills and/or acquire the resources necessary. How could you get there? Perhaps break your bigger goal into smaller "bite size" ones and chew on them first. Sometimes we set goals that are hard to attain and get frustrated along the way when we feel we aren't getting anywhere, but that doesn't mean we shouldn't stretch ourselves in some ways to feel challenged.

You also need to think how RELEVANT or realistic the goal is to you. This is the tricky part of the SMART goal process, but it's of significant importance to think it through. You need to ask yourself if the goal make sense at this very stage in your personal or professional life? How will it affect your day-to-day life and is that worth it? What are the benefits? Does the goal align with your values? Does it fit into your overall vision? If you determine the goal is just a sudden urge or an irrational desire, scratch it from your list and come up with one that actually matters to you and will help you in creating the life you want to live.

Each goal needs to be TIME-ORIENTED in that it has a start and finish date, otherwise you lose the sense of urgency and your motivation to achieve it. So always ask yourself when you will start and when you will complete your goal.

Once you have established a goal, it's very important to keep your WHY front and center. I touched on that in Chapter 4. You need to know why you are doing what you are doing and why you are pursuing the goals you set to achieve. Your WHY makes the goal clear and it moves, drives, and energizes you. Your WHY gives meaning to everything you do and helps you get back up when you get knocked off your feet. So, as you make your goals and action plans, revisit your WHY every so often as a way of reconnecting with your purpose (and therefore motivation) behind it all. When Jack and I ran into roadblocks and challenges while refitting our boat, we reminded each other of our passion and desire to build a business together, which was and still is our WHY and has kept us going despite the struggles we've encountered along the way.

You also want to review likely obstacles. What obstacles might you face that could stop you? This is all about setting yourself up for success and anticipating what you may need. Again, it's something Jack and I have done while planning the refit, and we continue to do while working on our business plan for the future. We do research all the time. We talk about possible roadblocks and how to deal with them.

It's prep work! Remember, there is a difference between planning for possible roadblocks compared to worrying about them. The advantage of planning is you can manage problems more quickly and efficiently, because you will be ready to implement the solutions you already have at hand.

Now that we've talked about how to set SMART goals let's look at how to accomplish them, which is the next step in getting closer to what you want to achieve and/or have in your life. This is where systems and routines come into play. As I mentioned earlier systems and routines help us to stay organized and focused, create time to do what's important to us, build better habits and stay on track. In today's world, it's easy to get distracted and off track. So many things scream for our attention, whether it's work, family, friends, obligations, social media, the news, cell phones, tablets, computers, and the like. How can we stay focused and make progress on our goals if we get distracted all day long?

It's important to remember the distractions are not the real problem, it's the way we deal with them. If we let them get a hold of us, we lose control of our attention – the attention we need to focus on our goals. A system helps you to maintain control of your day, your goals, and priorities, and it can help you organize your time in the most efficient way. Without a system or a plan of action, it's easy to create voids that get quickly filled by all the distractions that are just waiting to solicit your time and attention.

What's the best system to follow? The most powerful system is the one you create for yourself. The one that works for you. You can use the help of "performance planners," which are readily available today and can help as a guideline. But at the end, it's your way that matters. By creating your own plan of action, you become intentional as to where and how you invest and focus your time and energy. By doing so, it's far more likely you will achieve the results you want. I have developed many systems over time, for business as well as personal goals and love doing it because I know systems and routines are roadmaps to success. It's like designing a railroad track that your train can travel along. By designing yourself a track, you are laying out the principles of what you want to do and when you are going to do it. Let me share with you a simple framework you can follow when developing your action-oriented plans.

PUTTING THIS TOOL INTO ACTION

Step 1. Goal-Setting

1. Write down all the goals you currently have (whether they are short term or long term goals), each on its own index card. This way you can work with them as you please and add to your list at any time. If you have a huge audacious goal (like immigrating to another country or re-fitting a boat like I did), you might find it helpful to break it down into smaller chunks so you can get started and see meaningful progress right away. I like to use the old-fashioned pen and paper to start with as it creates a tactile connection. You can always transfer to electronics later, such as a Trello Board.

2. Next pick one to three goals for this year that would make it the best year ever. You could also go month by month and pick a short-term goal that if achieved would make the next month the best month ever. Follow the SMART approach Specific, Measurable, Achievable, Realistic, and Time-Oriented. Make sure the goals align with your values. Write down your WHY next to each goal. Remember that's your motivator and will help you to push through hard times.

3. For each goal, write down the action steps you need to take to achieve the particular goal – you can use the back of the index card. Depending on the goal, the list might require just a few tasks or it can be a long list of things to do. Don't worry about organizing any of it at this point or missing a step or two, just squeeze out your brain and write down whatever comes up around that particular goal. Think of what needs to get handled, what are specific to-do items, what decisions need to be made, what conversations or communications might need to take place and so forth. Brain dump first, then organize!

4. Now try to organize your action steps in order of importance. For example, this needs to be done immediately or today, this needs to be next, and that can be done any time this week, etc. Again, do not worry about what's missing or inaccurate, it will come to you as you start working on the project.

I work with SMART GOALS all the time. I've used them when building my coaching practice, Jack and I used them when selling our house and building our charter business, and I used them while writing this book.

Step 2. Block out time for your goals and yourself.

Time blocking puts you in control of your schedule, so your schedule doesn't control you. You are setting clear and concrete guidelines on when and how long you'll work on what. When you schedule out chunks of time in advance to work on a specific project or task, you are more likely to follow through versus having vague intentions. If you are the type of person that really bristles with this type of structure, I encourage you to think about how your current scheduling/habits are working for you. If they work for you and you get results, great, keep on doing what you are doing. If they don't work, try time blocking, it works! If I don't block out specific times for specific projects, something else will come in between and I will not get done what's truly important to me.

Either on Sundays or each Monday morning, dedicate about 20 to 30 minutes to schedule out the week and determine what days you could add a block of time to work on your goals. Even a small block of time is better than no time at all. Now block out the time, and treat it as a non-negotiable appointment. That's the key element here! When the time comes, put yourself in "airplane mode" and be "unreachable." This is crucial and requires focus and determination, but you will do it if you truly want to make progress on your goals. It means blocking out all possible distractions – like your cell phone or email notifications - and fully concentrating on the task at hand. Tell others, such as your family or co-workers, about your sacred block of time and ask them to support you by not disturbing you.

When you work on your goal, look at your to-do list and start with the highest priority and give it all you've got in the time you have. There is an enormous amount of power in focusing on just one thing at a time instead of multi-tasking. Work your way down the list from the highest priority to the lowest until your time is up for the day. Come back to finish when your next time block for that particular project shows up on your calendar.

Also, don't forget to block out time for your empowering morning routine. As I mentioned in Chapter 4, practicing a morning routine not only makes you feel good about yourself, but it will also assist you in focusing on your goals. It comes back to choices and decision making. "Where there is a will there's a way!" You are in control.

You may feel stuck or fight the thought of finding the time to work on your goals or morning routine because your calendar seems stuffed already. If you find yourself in level 1 or 2, victim or fighting energy mode, work your way mentally up the ladder and see if you can adopt a different thought and approach that works better for you.

Step 3. Set Boundaries and Start Saying "No"

This step is one of the most powerful and often gets overlooked. I've touched on it in Chapter 6 and promised to come back to it with a plan on how to build your "No System".

Learning to say "no" can be a big challenge with all the endless opportunities that get thrown at us on a daily basis, yet it's crucial. In order to make time for what's most important to you, and what adds value to your life, you might need to say "no" to more things. Think about your day and what you engage in. What are your weak spots, activities that suck you into "lala-land?" Is it social media, television, games, emailing, texting, non-essential phone calls, appointments, projects, outings? Are you saying "yes" to a whole bunch of people and committing yourself to things because you like to help out or simply because you like to socialize? There is nothing wrong with being a social butterfly, and helping others is great. We just need to put it all into perspective and evaluate where we can free up time to create balance and work on what matters most to us.

Looking at the activities that take up your time, ask yourself what you want to say "no" to next week so you can gain time for yourself. It can help doing a time/day inventory to see where you actually spend your time. It gives objectivity! You might be surprised by how much time you spent in one area. It also helps to start in small doses saying "no." If social media is where you spend hours of time each day, reduce the amount of time or schedule a time block for social media activity. You could also set a time or time intervals to check your email and return phone calls versus picking up the phone every time it rings or notifies you of a new email or text. It's something I started doing. It's helped me especially while writing this book. You can turn off the notification function on your phone or computer. Each day and each week consider "what matters the least should not get in the way of what matters the most!" Saying "no" to small or trivial things puts you in control so you can start living your life the way you want it!

Step 4. Create a Daily VIT (Very Important Task)

Before I go to bed each night, I pick one thing on my list for the next day that becomes my VIT, my very important task for the day. That VIT takes priority over all other activities. It's a task that is goal-oriented and of value to me. While I always strive to accomplish the things I set to achieve each day, I pick one for the day that is precious to me and that I will not compromise no matter what. Why do I do this? No matter how crazy my day is going to be, at the end of it I can feel victorious having at least worked on my VIT, which is better than feeling that the day took over and I've accomplished nothing. Sound familiar? Try VITing. Some days my VIT can be as simple as drinking three 24-oz bottles of water or taking a walk for half an hour. Another day it might be completing one specific task on my never-ending to-do list such as scraping and sanding the arch on our boat, doing bookkeeping for at least one hour, or working on my website for a certain period of time.

Step 5. Track your weekly progress.

Create a way to measure your performance each week. Why? It's another way of holding yourself accountable for what you say you'll do. Tracking your performance shows the progress you are making. When you see progress, you feel good about yourself, and it's easier to stay motivated. Tracking goes in line with the "Measurable" component of the SMART goal process. First you set qualifier or quantifier to measure your success, then you start tracking your performance. To help you with tracking, simply use any of the Track boards I've created over time. You'll find Performance as well as Goal Setting and Tracking Sheets on my website www.BreakLooseandFly.com under the Library Tab. Start there if you like and modify the worksheets as you see fit or make your own, whatever works best for you.

Tracking can be as complex or simple as you want to make it. I prefer simple as simple tends to get done more often. Tracking sheets create a very easy-to-digest documentation to verify whether you are accomplishing what you set out to do or not. It's not the same as having a calendar which tells you what to do each day and hour of the week; this is about providing a track record, an accountability tool, to show you the areas you want to work on based on the goals you set for yourself.

If you are "off," don't beat yourself up, just hop back on the train and keep following the tracks you laid. It's a guide to help you focus your attention, not a tool for self-punishment. Be flexible and move things around if they don't work out the way you intended. Tracking does not take much time and is so powerful because it keeps your awareness and focus on the things that are important to you. It's another way of living with intention.

While using tracking sheets is one way of checking your performance, I find it very helpful to have an accountability or performance partner for certain goals. Interestingly, we tend to be more accountable to someone else than to the person we see in the mirror. By letting someone else know what you are about to do and asking them to hold you accountable to it, you reach a higher level of motivation and are less likely to give up along the way. A partner can also help motivate, counsel, and coach as well as be a source for learning, feedback, and support. It's another thing Jack and I do; we hold each other accountable for what we say we'll do. That applies to our business as well as personal goals, like the intake of the oh so-yummy fermented grape juice that's not helpful while trying to lose weight. I am honest, I hate it when he reminds me of my goal wanting to lose weight while I pour myself a second glass of wine in the evening. But that's what an accountability partner is there for, to remind you of your goals, encourage you to stick with them, and support you in challenging times. Yup, it's challenging to pass up a treat! If that is something you are struggling with too, whether it's wine, chocolate, chips, or something else, you can see you are not alone! I am right with you!

The five steps above are a guideline you can follow for setting goals and implementing systems that will help you achieve your goals. Again, do it your way, do whatever works best for you. The important thing is to get a game plan together, and get moving on it. Don't procrastinate. The longer you wait to take action, the greater the odds are that you will never actually do it. Without action, there is no win or success. Putting a plan together may seem hard at first, but you'll get used to and even addicted to it once you find out you actually accomplish things with a written plan.

As much as I believe that setting goals, systems, and routines are vital to our success and get us closer to what we want, I also believe it's not necessarily the achievement of a particular goal that makes us successful. Success can be found in the journey itself. For me, success is learning something new each day, it's celebrating small wins, overcoming obstacles, not giving up when I am facing adversity, doing my best every day, living fully in the moment, being engaged, challenging myself, knowing where I am heading, believing I can do anything I put my mind to, overcoming fear and pushing through it. It's all those things and more. Sometimes we don't arrive at our planned destination, but it does not mean we failed. It just means we got derailed. Should that happen to you, know you are not alone and understand that your next step is to create a new action plan or modify the existing one so that you can continue moving forward.

Also, keep in mind a derailment is not necessarily a bad thing. Yes, it can be frustrating at first, but what if you find out later that the derailment took you to a new destination that's even better than the one you originally chose? When I found out the new business venture was collapsing under my feet, I was frustrated and bummed about it. My new action plan to become a coach and build a coaching practice got off track too when my husband informed me he was quitting his job and was going to buy a charter yacht. I guess I could have let him go on the journey by himself and keep doing what I was doing, but I decided to come along for the ride and build that new business together with him. As you know that only lasted until COVID hit and shut down that dream for both of us, which led to where I am today, writing this book. This whole series of events enabled me to see my true calling, which is being an author and sharing my experiences and knowledge as business manager and certified coach as well as my life experience, which alone is worth a couple novels.

Life is a journey, full of adventure, insights and aha moments. It offers us constant learning opportunities. With that I'd like to encourage you to not limit your version of success to the achievement of a goal, but to the journey itself. We each get to go on one journey, that's it. It's up to us what we make of it. Yes, the journey is not always pretty or comfortable and it will not conform to all that we desire, yet it can be beautiful, meaningful and fulfilling. We are responsible for the quality of our own journey − I am responsible for my journey; you alone are for yours. Alexandra Elle sums it up this way: "The sun will rise and set regardless. What we choose to do with the light while it's here is up to us. Journey wisely."

Here is your ACTION STEP for this tool.
Use it now!

Start tracking your progress. Remember, tracking your performance shows the progress you are making. When you see progress, you feel good about yourself, and it's easier to stay motivated.

Either use the Performance Tally Sheet from my website or simply use a pen and a piece of paper. Write a list of the activities or tasks you would like to complete this week. Write each activity or task on a separate line so you have space for tracking it.

Next to each of these line items put the number of times or hours you would like to allocate to each task/activity per week. As the week progresses, put a checkmark next to each line item as you accomplish either completing a task/activity or each hour you allocated to it. At the end of the week, do a tally to see how much time you actually spent on the things you set out to do. Remember, if you are "off," don't beat yourself up, just get back on the train and keep following the tracks you laid.

What activities will make it on your tracking sheet this week?

Everything you want is out there waiting for you to ask,
but you have to take action to get it.
~Jack Canfield

CHAPTER 10

Never Stop Listening, Learning, and Growing

Four years ago, I attended a yoga-centric "art of living retreat" my friend B. and her husband J. started offering in several countries. When they came to British Columbia, Canada, I took the opportunity and signed up because it was just a hop across the border from where I lived. Even though it stretched my pocketbook at the time, I signed up anyway because I had heard great things about their retreats, how they empower people to achieve their highest potential discovering happiness through an experience of detox, raw food, yoga, meditation, inner dance (which is a conscious trance meditation), nature, and adventure! I am always on the pursuit of personal growth, so the retreat sounded intriguing.

I was a bit nervous about the yoga portion of the retreat as I thought my stiff and broken body was simply not capable of performing the suggested moves. I have had many injuries including a fused vertebra, surgeries on both elbows, and broken wrists. Consequently, I can't flex my body freely and easily. So, I was concerned I would stick out like a sore thumb by not being able to do the exercises as gracefully as you see on TV or through studio windows. I was also nervous about immersing myself in long periods of meditation, which I had never done before. The thought of sitting still or laying down doing nothing or chanting mantras felt odd to me because that's something I had never done. I am always on the go. So, I knew there would be times I would feel uncomfortable, but I wanted to do it anyway.

Oh, boy, let me tell you, I had some stretching to do, like taking those three-minute cold showers first thing in the morning instead of my beloved ten-minute hot showers, drinking anti-inflammatory and immune system boosters like turmeric ginger cocktails on an empty stomach instead of coffee, or eating nothing but raw food throughout the day. There were other parts of the morning routine that felt a bit odd, like tongue cleansing, which is a traditional part of Ayurvedic self-care to prevent reabsorption of the toxins that form in your mouth and coat your tongue. Dry brushing your skin was also new to me, another part of ancient self-care practice to cleanse and beautify the skin, increase circulation, and make you feel invigorated and energized. And the yoga practices, oh dear, my stiff body left me dangling with my hands at my knees while everyone else was bending their bodies like gummy bears. I couldn't hold a pose for very long either without falling over. If you are someone who gets discouraged because you can only touch your toes while bending your knees 45 degrees, you'll understand what I mean.

I felt that I stood out like a sore thumb among all these yogis, just as I expected. Every time I looked through the room and compared myself to what everyone else was capable of doing, I felt myself drifting into "self-pity land." This retreat took place prior to my going through the coaching program, so I wasn't as skilled in working myself out of the "victim/feeling sorry for myself" mode as I am today. I ended up lingering in it several times over the course of the retreat. I didn't like it.

One time, I got so upset not being able to bend freely like the others that I ran out of the yoga practice and started bawling. I felt so out of place, I could not help myself but cry. Yup, there I was, the ox that usually plows through the fields no matter how hard the ground is, but something as "simple" as not being able to participate in yoga like everyone else brought me to tears. What self-pity can do to you, eh?

As challenging as parts of the retreat were, I am grateful I pushed myself to learn new methods that helped me recharge my batteries both mentally, physically, and emotionally. I left the retreat rejuvenated, energized, new and improved, and determined to continue what we practiced because I experienced the benefits of it (including the benefits of meditation and how it can reduce stress in the body and mind). Wow, what a discovery! The more I committed to my own personal development, the more that commitment did its magic, and the more I got out of it.

Two years later, my friends were back in Canada offering another retreat. I thought of joining them again as I sadly had gained 20 pounds and felt exhausted at the end of each day. The "warning light" had come on telling me to take better care of myself and to not let life's circumstances shape me in a way that was dissatisfying to me. I determined that another energy booster was warranted and another reminder of what's truly important in my life, which is my health and well-being. Without that, I can't accomplish anything.

This time I approached the retreat with a whole different mindset, because of the training I had received from becoming a certified coach and learning about Energy Leadership. I was not going to let self-pity take over again. I was determined to move myself out of this destructive type of energy as quickly as possible and tap into the higher levels that are growth oriented.

We started the four-day journey with an "opening circle" where we each shared our intentions, why we joined the retreat, and what we wanted to get out of it. Next, we were asked to draw a Zen card that would be our companion for the weekend and perhaps bring joy, inspiration, or a new level of awareness into our lives. I drew "comparison." Wow, what a match for me. Perhaps it was time for me to revisit the subject with my new and improved way of approaching the world.

I took the long weekend to think about the meaning of "comparison." When we compare ourselves to the people around us, we either consciously or subconsciously judge and determine who holds the longer or the shorter end of the stick. Comparing ourselves to others either genetically, like in the way we look, or in how capable we are of doing something is dangerous. It's a recipe for unhappiness if we determine, in our mind, that we are holding the short end of the stick. Thinking of yourself as less mature, less gifted, less flexible, less recognized, less capable, and so forth feeds your anxiety, insecurities, and self-doubt, which leads to discouragement, envy, and potentially preventing yourself from moving forward toward any of your goals. You know the drill.

On the other hand, thinking of yourself as superior in comparison to others promotes pride and ego, which can also be destructive because you constantly subject yourself to the danger of falling from your own subjective opinion of yourself. Further, you are potentially creating a wall between you and those you interact with daily, if through your body language and attitude you make them feel inferior or give them the feeling you feel superior to them.

The interesting thing about comparison is it's in the eye of the beholder how someone or something is seen or perceived. Like the old saying, "One person's weed is another person's flower." While you might see yourself as a weed, another person might think of you as a flower. So, the whole comparison idea is fruitless, because the answers are subject to the judgment of the person comparing.

So, why do we do it? There is no need. We are all incomparable and unique. Whether or not we can bend our bodies like gummy bears doing yoga does not define us. What defines us is whether we try bending our body or not, doing our best despite the fact it may be hard and uncomfortable, and staying true to ourselves with all the perfections and imperfections we have. My Zen card truly enlightened me and helped me to focus my energy on my capabilities and how I could improve myself without getting caught up in what the others were doing.

Each morning we would meet down at the lake dressed in our bathing suits and wrapped in towels. The idea was to replace the three-minute cold morning shower I was used to from the previous retreat with a three-minute plunge in the lake. *Seriously*, I thought, *that's a bit much to ask on a cold September morning in the Pacific Northwest.* While I was debating how to approach the challenge, I watched all the other participants jump off the dock into the lake, arms up in the air yelling a "hu-ha" or whatever they felt like before submerging into the cold water. "Cold water shock" went through my mind. I thought, *I am not conditioned for that, let's walk into the lake to give my body a chance to acclimate to the cold temperature.* I heard my friend asking, "Is Kerstin in the water yet?" On that note, I rushed to the water's edge and walked in as quickly as possible to avoid being singled out. Holy moly, talk about subjecting yourself to the uncomfortable. It was a true challenge and a long three minutes where I had to force myself to stay put and concentrate on the "health benefits of cold water plunging." When it was time to get out, I emerged with a wide smile having been able to participate with all the gummy bears in their game. Victory, yeah. It was hard, but I was excited. I pushed through the discomfort of plunging into a cold lake in September in British Columbia, Canada.

Kundalini yoga was next on the agenda. I took the energy level 3 and 4 approach right from the start. My level 3 "Rationalizer" approach was "I am in control of my life, I know how to play the game, the way I see myself is completely up to me, I can do better than last time." My level 4 "Caregiver" approach was "I am here to nourish my body and my soul, I will strive to do my best, I am worth it." Wow, what a difference it made for me to focus on those thoughts. Whenever I caught myself looking through the room comparing my capabilities to the others, I thought *no, let's not go there, this is the wrong way, concentrate on what you can do and how you can improve.* I thought of stair-stepping my way through the poses I was not able to do and decided to begin with the "bend over and touch your toes" pose, because it was a true challenge for me with my fused vertebrae. Touching my toes was too far of a reach for the weekend, but going halfway down my shin seemed achievable. I remembered that in the last retreat I thought, *I wish I could, but I simply can't.* This time around I chose to think *let's see how much further I can bend down by just trying.* Wow, I was surprised my body seemed more cooperative with that new frame of mind and my pushing myself. Every time I was able to bend down a bit more than the day before, I caught myself smiling, thinking *yeah, my body is able to do way more than I think it can.* That thought and feeling encouraged me to try harder to see how much more my body would give me if I just gave it a chance instead of thinking *I can't do it.* I didn't quite reach my goal for the weekend, but I was on my way and determined to get there with practice.

On the last day of the retreat, my friends put something really special on the program.

Ice bathing!

Apparently, the cold-water swimming wasn't enough every morning. Now we were supposed to immerse ourselves into a bathtub filled to the top with nothing but ice cubes, and sit in it for three full minutes!

I don't have any masochistic tendencies. Something like this would never even cross my mind, neither in a wetsuit nor naked, so I would not be easily convinced to participate. Ice bathing was not on my bucket list or my list of brave things to do. I put my bathing suit on anyway and gathered around the tub with the others. *I can at least be present for the ceremony* went through my mind, even though the thought of standing around the tub, barely dressed on a cold afternoon did not appeal to me either. Aack! As everyone took a turn stepping into the tub, submerging into the ice cubes all the way up to their shoulders, the rest of us moved our arms and bodies singing hu-ha the entire three minutes to support the person in the tub while my friend J was playing the drums and singing ancient words sending good vibes to the ice bather.

Everyone else had gone and all eyes were on me. Have you ever experienced that? I call it informal persuasion through peer pressure, which can be great when learning new healthy habits, or not so great when following the group down a path that could be harmful. As I scrambled for a positive empowering thought, "courage" came to mind. Courage is the ability to do something that frightens you. Courage is feeling the fear and doing it anyway. Okay, *how can I do it?* went through my mind. I thought about making it a game to see who wins, the fear or me. I like to turn challenges into games. It's more motivating for me to "attack" them. So, I said "hello" to the fear, rubbed my hands together. and thought *bring it on, let's get the show on the road, we'll see who is stronger. I know I CAN DO IT; I just need to push myself.* I knew fear only existed in my head, it's a thought that triggers feelings of discomfort. It was up to me to choose to chicken out or embrace the feeling of fear, acknowledge it exists only in my mind, and courageously climb into the tub. So, I climbed in the tub.

The pain was excruciating. I gasped for air. My brain and every cell in my body screamed to get the heck out of the tub. However, my friends and the others helped me stay focused. Believe it or not, while the first two seconds and then two minutes were torture, the last minute was bearable. I couldn't feel my body anymore. The sting had disappeared. I was able to force a smile for the camera.

Emerging from the ice was amazing. I felt immensely powerful and strong. This is what I meant earlier when I said, "greatness awaits on the other side of fear." The mental strength I gained from this experience made me think and feel herculean because I was able to push through the self-imposed barrier of thinking I couldn't survive the ice plunge. I was so proud of myself. It's one of the greatest feelings in the world. If you too can accomplish similar feats, you'll discover new doors opening for you.

It's experiences like this that compel me to invest my time and money in workshops, seminars, conferences, training, and programs that focus on personal development and skill building to better my game. I would not have tackled the ice bath by myself nor think of such challenge to gain more strength. But by surrounding myself with powerful people, I am able to push myself beyond of what I think I am capable of and level up my game. The energy that comes from a room filled with "big thinkers and movers" can truly light a fire in you and level up your own game as well.

Every hour and dollar I've spent on pursuing personal growth has given me greater return than expected, like Benjamin Franklin once said, "For the best return on your money, pour your purse into your head." I've done that quite a few times, not just my head, but my heart and whole being, and I don't regret it. I found by listening to and learning from people living a life of excellence or who are doing what you want to do, you can:

- Experience multiple Aha-Moments
- Receive Guidance and Strategies to better your Game
- Get Motivated and Inspired
- Improve your Mindset to be able to move Mountains
- Turn Fear into Power
- Develop Relationships to network and keep yourself accountable

If you are tired of living a stagnate life or feel stuck on the hamster wheel, it's time to pound your fist on the table and say, "Enough. I am done living like that, I want more, I want better and I want it now." If you feel that way, awesome. Let's get you moving! Here is one more tool that will help you to create your amazing life.

TOOL #10: Invest in Yourself through Personal Development

"Personal Development" is the conscious pursuit of growth by improving self-awareness and developing skills to maximize your potential so you can become the best you can be. It's a transformational process. By changing your "inside world" and becoming the best version of yourself, you are able to change your "outside world" and enhance the quality of your life. That's why I invest time and money in outside resources such as books, workshops, coaching, and retreats. In today's world, online programs are a big part of my education. Surrounding myself with like-minded people who aspire to live their best lives is a great way to learn new things and feel inspired. It's the key tool to better your game, just like the chef's knife is the key tool in a professional kitchen.

When I was training to be a chef on our chartered yacht, I learned to care for my main knife deeply and sharpen it frequently. It is used in the most important cut and the sharper the knife the better the cuts, which in turn ensure more visually appealing dishes. This not only applies to the chef knife, but it also applies to the assortment of knives a chef needs to be able to perform well in the kitchen. Some knives however play a more important role, just like ingredients, others are more supportive, but all have an impact on the chef's performance and the end product, which you'll see and get to taste if you go out for dinner. So, when thinking about the tools in this book, think in terms of an assortment of knives a chef has in his kitchen to perform best. Your main knife is your personal development, your supporting knifes are the nine tools I previously shared with you.

Here is the critical point though. All the knives in your drawer, like all the tools in this book don't do you any good if you don't use them. Implementation of what you've learned is what will make a difference in your life.

Use the Tools in this Book

The ten tools we explored are here in your hands to help you grow and create a life you will love. But there are many more tools out there ready for you to discover. Place the ones that work for you in your toolbox for life, and add new tools as you find them throughout your discovery journey. Most importantly, **USE THEM!** There's a vast difference between knowing what to do versus actually doing it. We can be well-educated, but if we don't put our knowledge to work, it's unlikely we will see the changes we desire. So, treat yourself with love and the utmost respect, nourish your body and soul. Invest in your personal development and pursue it. You are worth it! Execution is where the rubber meets the road. Acting versus dreaming and hoping is what separates the people who live a life they love from those that wish they were living a life they would love. Don't join those that live with regrets and wish they would have acted sooner. Act now, you only get to live once and time is ticking, so do it, whatever it may be, just **DO IT!**

Let me ask you one question. Do you think that if you implemented the tools in this book and took the steps I've taken myself to break through barriers that were holding me back, you could get unstuck, embrace challenges and navigate through them, act with more courage, take more changes, conquer your self-limiting beliefs and transform your life so you can live it to the fullest? I hope your answer is yes, because you actually could! It is possible!!! Even if you start out using just one or two of the tools, it can take your ordinary life to extraordinary and the more you choose to adapt, the greater the extraordinary can be. It's your choice!

The tools may sound simple and they actually are, that's what I love about them. Simple, but powerful! Everybody can use them to improve their lives, you included. I've identified my key wins from each. Now it's your turn to sort through, prioritize and put into place the ones that work for you. We call it *mise en place*. It's a French culinary phrase and refers to putting everything into place before starting to cook, ingredients as well as tools. So, *mise en place* your tools and strategies, **USE THEM** and get ready to change your life!

Are you ready?

Will you choose today as the day to get serious about your personal development and goals? Will you take action to become all you are capable of becoming? Moving is the key element here, no matter how fast or slow you go. Just move. Don't allow fear and self-doubt to guide you to the nearest exit. Stay on your tracks. Live your life, engage and shape it the way you want it to be. YOU CAN DO IT. You are far more powerful than you allow yourself to be.

Marianne Williamson writes, "Our deepest fear is not that we are inadequate, our deepest fear is that we are powerful beyond measure. It is our light, not our darkness, that most frightens us."

The later part of her poem says we are all meant to shine, and the glory of God is within all of us, in you and in me. "And as we let our own light shine, we unconsciously give other people permission to do the same." This is a human characteristic called "mirroring." Have you ever noticed when a really happy person enters the room? The room becomes happier. Or when a really grumpy person enters the room? Negative energy seems to take over. This phenomenon is created unconsciously. With training such as that provided by Energy Leadership, we can react consciously to these circumstances. This allows us to let our light shine no matter what energy surrounds us. Energy Leadership helps us develop an effective style by which we live our lives that positively influences and changes us, and those around us through "positive" mirroring. Think about becoming the "shining" mirror in the room. With practice you can walk into a negative environment and change the tone through your inner strength to maintain a positive demeanor and attitude regardless of the situation. How would that feel?

As you take this journey through personal development and begin crafting a life to the level of success and satisfaction you have defined for yourself, use the following tips to put the personal development tool in your favor. I touched on these points before, but would like to reiterate them in this summary to emphasize their importance:

PUTTING THIS TOOL INTO ACTION

- **Start where you are.** Don't let that voice in your head dictate to you that you can't start to change your life because you are not capable or not worth it. That voice is wrong and has no business to tell you anything!!! You are worth it and capable just the way you are at this moment in time! Perhaps you are a bit shaky at how you fly your plane, but that skill can be improved. All it takes at the outset is to actually start and not come up with any excuses why you can't or why you need to wait. Wait for what? You've got nothing to lose, only to gain! Start now!

- **Take one step at the time.** I've talked about stair-stepping earlier in this chapter. Break your goals into smaller bite size steps and attempt the "staircase" one step at a time. It's more attainable this way and you can see meaningful progress right away. That motivates! So, don't look at the mountain in front of you, just focus on the next step that's necessary to get you moving forward. If you think you can't take the next step, you most likely won't. Remember, your thoughts, trigger your emotions and your emotions trigger your actions. If you think and tell your mind you can and you will take the next step, your feet will move!

- **Don't compare yourself to others** and wish you had what they have, whether it's their looks, capabilities, friends, or money. Remember, comparing yourself to others is a recipe for unhappiness if you, in your mind, hold the short end of the yardstick. It's such an easy trap to fall into. Don't do it. Focus your energy on what you are capable of now and how you can improve.

- **Hold on to your values and stay true to yourself.** We talked about that in Chapter 5. Whatever you decide to do, choose actions that are aligned with your values and connect you to your deeper Why. Be you, not like someone else likes you to be or you think you need to be. You don't have to prove yourself to anyone. You are you, stay true to your own personality, your spirit, your character. That makes you unique! Determine what it is that you want, what's important to you, then take a stand and have the courage to claim it!

- **Never stop listening and learning.** Seek and surround yourself with people who have already done what it is you want to do and pay close attention to what you can take away from their stories, tips, and advice. Adopt the tools or parts that work for you. If your budget allows, sign up for workshops, seminars or retreats, get a coach and if that's unfeasible read books and listen to podcasts and the like, to widen your knowledge base. There is a lot of free information out there that successful people are willing to share. Knowledge is power and when you feel empowered you are able to make the desired changes in your life.

- **Challenge yourself.** Stretch yourself to feel challenged and do what's uncomfortable, push through the discomfort and you'll come out the other side a different person. It only feels wrong at the start because we all have an automatic attraction toward the easier way. If you take the easy route you are denying yourself the satisfaction of achievement. It's amazing what you can discover by challenging yourself!

- **Be accountable**. Hold yourself accountable for what you say you'll do. Actions will get you results. You are responsible to initiate and perform the steps necessary to get you closer to where you want to be. If you don't bother, no one else will. Tip, you can use your friends as accountability partners by simply telling them your plans. I find this to be one of the most powerful tools in my toolbox, self-inflicted peer pressure to better yourself.

- **Be consistent.** I can't say it better than Tony Robbins: "In essence, if we want to direct our lives, we must take control of our consistent actions. It's not what we do once in a while that shapes our lives, but what we do consistently."

• **Watch your "consumption,"** consume wisely and eliminate, reduce, or avoid those things or people that don't serve you well, rob you of your precious time, and/or poison your thoughts and feelings. Negative vibes are equally as contagious as positive ones, watch who you spend your time with, and who (or what) you are listening to. Always ask yourself, "is what I am paying attention to supporting my pursuit of personal growth or is it holding me back?"

• **Practice Courage.** Yes, you can practice it, just like I did when facing the ice tub plunge. Play the "I've got courage game" I described earlier in this chapter. After reading this book I hope you understand you can choose to let fear impact you and stop you from acting or you can choose to courageously act, push through fear and come out the winner. No matter what the actual outcome is, you will be the winner because you acted and faced your fear, you did not let it stop you. That's winning as far as I'm concerned!

• **Never ever give up or stop trying.** Developing better habits to get you in shape both physically and mentally takes training and time. Staying in shape is a lifetime endeavor. If you fall short in your training or get bruised along the way, know you are not alone as this happens to many of us. Get your eyes off of the failure or setback and fix them again on your target as described in Chapter 4. Get up, dust yourself off, shift gears, and get going again putting your best effort to the task at hand. It's not what happens to us that determines the major outcome in our life, it's how we respond and how we let it impact us. Confucius says it best, "Our greatest glory is not in never failing, but in rising every time we fall." As I said it before, falling is part of growing and becoming better. I truly believe for every challenge encountered there is an opportunity for growth.

- **Enjoy the journey.** That is in my opinion the most important thing. I don't just want to be happy upon my arrival, I want to be happy every day I am on the road. And to be happy, content, and fulfilled I am taking the tools I've come to learn over the years with me and I use them to help me feel great, and conquer roadblocks and challenges as quickly as possible. I collect new tools whenever I find them and try them out to see how and in what way they can support me in my endeavor to become the best version of myself and create the amazing life I want to live.

Ideally life would be simply wonderful every day, but you and I know that not all days are sunny and warm. Sometimes it rains and sometimes it storms. It's not that we can avoid these days, but we can be better prepared to handle them with bravery, courage, and strength. These traits don't come naturally for many of us, we have to invest time, energy, and effort to develop those skills so we can perform our best each time we face unbearable weather. We need to put our working gear on and start hammering away whether it's sunny or stormy outside. Every so often I get a comment from clients or people I talk to like "oh it sounds so easy and for you it seems to work."

Well, my friend, I have not once in this book said it's easy, other than tracking your performance on a sheet of paper, and it only works for me because I keep working on it all the time. I never stop listening, learning, practicing, and improving. Some days are absolutely amazing, some are just okay, and some are hard. But no matter how easy and wonderful, or how difficult and challenging the days are, I keep hammering away to become better every day and make my life the best it can be. If I fall short of the things I set out to do, I look in the mirror and tell the person I see to get with it and start moving again. When I feel down or discouraged, I find something to be grateful for and I'll come up with an affirmation that empowers me to move on, like "I can and I will push through this..." Gratitude and Affirmations are my most powerful tools, I use them all the time. If you don't know where to start, start working with those and you'll be amazed how much they can change your world for the better.

Are you ready to change your world and embark on the journey toward your dreams and goals? Are you ready to jump off of your secure "branch" to spread your wings and try flying?

Jump my friend, in the face of fear and "you will find out how to unfold your wings as you fall" as Ray Bradbury would say it. I know this statement is true, because I experienced it many times in my life. Taking a leap of faith and jumping in the unknown more than once has gotten me to where I am today. I love where I am, but I know there is more for me to experience and discover, so I'll keep on jumping to explore all that life has to offer me.

Before I leave you with one last exercise, I'd like to share something I overheard while standing on the pier in Naples, Florida. My husband and I were mesmerized watching the pelicans dive bomb head–first into the water to catch fish. A guy walking by us said, "Those birds are committed while we go to the convenience store." Wow. What a powerful statement. The parable stuck with me while I kept watching the birds. Some of the pelicans were successful, others not. The ones that caught a fish were swimming along munching on their catch, the ones that didn't catch a fish just took a moment to regain their strength, then lifted their large bodies back up in the air with huge strokes of their wings to dive bomb again. They did this over and over until they were successful. True commitment until they got what they were after!

How committed are you to your goals and how hard are you willing to work to get what you want?

"By changing your "inside" world and becoming the best version of yourself you are able to change your "outside" world and enhance the quality of your life."

~Kerstin Decook

Here is your ACTION STEP for this tool.
Use it now!

Take a 3-minute ice bath. Just kidding!

Identify one weakness you have that is a constraint to you achieving a specific goal, like smoking too many cigarettes when you like to stop smoking, spending too much time on social media or staying up too late watching movies, thus not being able to get up early and work on your empowering morning routine, and the likes, you get the idea.

Now, think of a first step on the stairway to your goal you could apply in the next seven days to get you one step closer to your goal. If you like, find an accountability partner that will cheer you on and support you. Next create yourself a success tracking sheet (or use mine from the Library) for that one to-do and commit on doing it, every day starting today for the next week. Think of an Affirmation that can help you each day to stick to your goal, like "I am more than capable of changing old habits to new ones that support my success. I can do it, I just need to start" Or you can come up with a statement directly related to your weakness, write it down on your tracking sheet and also on a sticky note, then stick the note where you'll see it before you give in to the weakness… on the fridge, on the wine cabinet, on the bedside table, on the TV remote, etc. to keep it at the forefront of your mind. Give it all you've got, like your life depends on it. You've got this, you are capable and you are worth the effort!!! When the week is over, tally up and decide whether to repeat or move on. Repetition is a key learning aid to help form new habits and skills. Give yourself time, but don't give in. Keep moving even if you slipped. When you think you mastered the first step and are ready to take on more, find the next step to climb. That's how you start creating a life you love, one step at a time.

What first step will you take, my dear friend?

We learn to fly not by being fearless, but by the daily practice of courage.
~Sam Keen

APPENDIX

Before we part, I would like to leave you with a poem I found online. Unfortunately, I don't know who to give credit as the author is unknown, but the message rings clear in my heart as to what I want to share with you. I hope you enjoy this poem and please don't be a stranger to what lies ahead of you in this wonderful world we all share.

As You Travel Through Life
Author Unknown

As you travel through life there are always those times
When decisions just have to be made,
When the choices are hard, and solutions seem scarce,
And the rain seems to soak your parade.

There are some situations where all you can do
Is simply let go and move on,
Gather your courage and choose a direction
That carries you toward a new dawn.

So pack up your troubles and take a step forward –
The process of change can be tough,
But think about all the excitement ahead

There might be adventures you never imagined
Just waiting around the next bend,
And wishes and dreams just about to come true
In ways you can't yet comprehend!

Perhaps you'll find friendships
that spring from new things
As you challenge your status quo,
And learn there are so many options in life,

Perhaps you'll go places you never expected
And see things that you've never seen,
Or travel to fabulous, faraway worlds
And wonderful spots in between!

Perhaps you'll find warmth and affection and caring
And somebody special who's there
To help you stay centered and listen with interest
To stories and feelings you share.

Perhaps you'll find comfort in knowing your friends
Are supportive of all that you do,
And believe that whatever decisions you make,
They'll be the right choices for you.

So keep putting one foot in front of the other,
And taking your life day by day...
There's a brighter tomorrow that's just down the road –
Don't look back! You're not going that way!

RESOURCES

If you are interested in a list of the books I've read to widen my knowledge and hone my skills to master life's challenges and create the amazing life I am living today, visit my website www.Breaklooseandfly. com and check the Library tab. My book resource list is constantly growing, so if you like up-to-date information, my website is the best place to get it and the worksheets I talked about earlier. If you are curious about what your "energetic makeup" looks like in daily life versus when you are under stress, you can order your personal Energy Leadership Index Assessment together with a debrief session on my website as well.

I am developing workshops and seminars related to subjects in this book and will post those to the site when available. If there is anything else I can help you with, please feel free to connect with me, and let's tackle your stuff together.

ABOUT THE AUTHOR

Kerstin Decook was born and raised in Russian-occupied Eastern Germany. While growing up "behind the wall" was incredibly challenging, she never stopped dreaming about being free one day and able to do what she wanted to do. This dream and many more came alive, but not without her facing seemingly insurmountable hurdles—social, emotional, personal, and economic. She never gave up and managed to navigate through all of them. She became a Social Educator, immigrated to North America at the age of 27 with limited knowledge of English, successfully created and managed Real Estate sales teams, raised two children, achieved Certified Professional Coach (CPC) and Energy Leadership Index Master Practitioner (ELI-MP) designations, and re-invented herself to be First Mate and Chef de Cuisine during  the summer season on the small adventure charter yacht she and her husband Jack own and operate in the Pacific Northwest. Lately, she added "author" to her list of careers.

Educating and supporting others has always been and still is Kerstin's greatest passion. She loves sharing her knowledge and experience to help others improve their lives, regardless of their circumstances. Her book *Break Loose and Fly* was born from that passion. When not writing, cruising, cooking, or polishing their boat, you may find Kerstin doing workshops and seminars, coaching, digging in her garden, spending time with family and friends, or traveling around the globe.

Want to connect with Kerstin? Visit her website at www.breaklooseandfly.com.

Will You Post a Review at Your Favorite Online Retailer?

If you like what you read in *Break Loose and Fly*, please post an honest review. My book is available at Amazon.com and Barnes & Noble. This will help me reach more people with this message. Thank you.

BREAK LOOSE AND FLY
COACHING

Mailing Address
Break Loose and Fly Coaching LLC
PO BOX 30308
Bellingham, WA 98228

Email
kd@breaklooseandfly.com

Website
www.breaklooseandfly.com

Social Media
Facebook - www.facebook.com/breaklooseandfly
LinkedIn - www.linkedin.com/in/kerstin-decook-29a1b1152
Instagram - www.instagram.com/breaklooseandflycoaching/